Y0-ASP-124

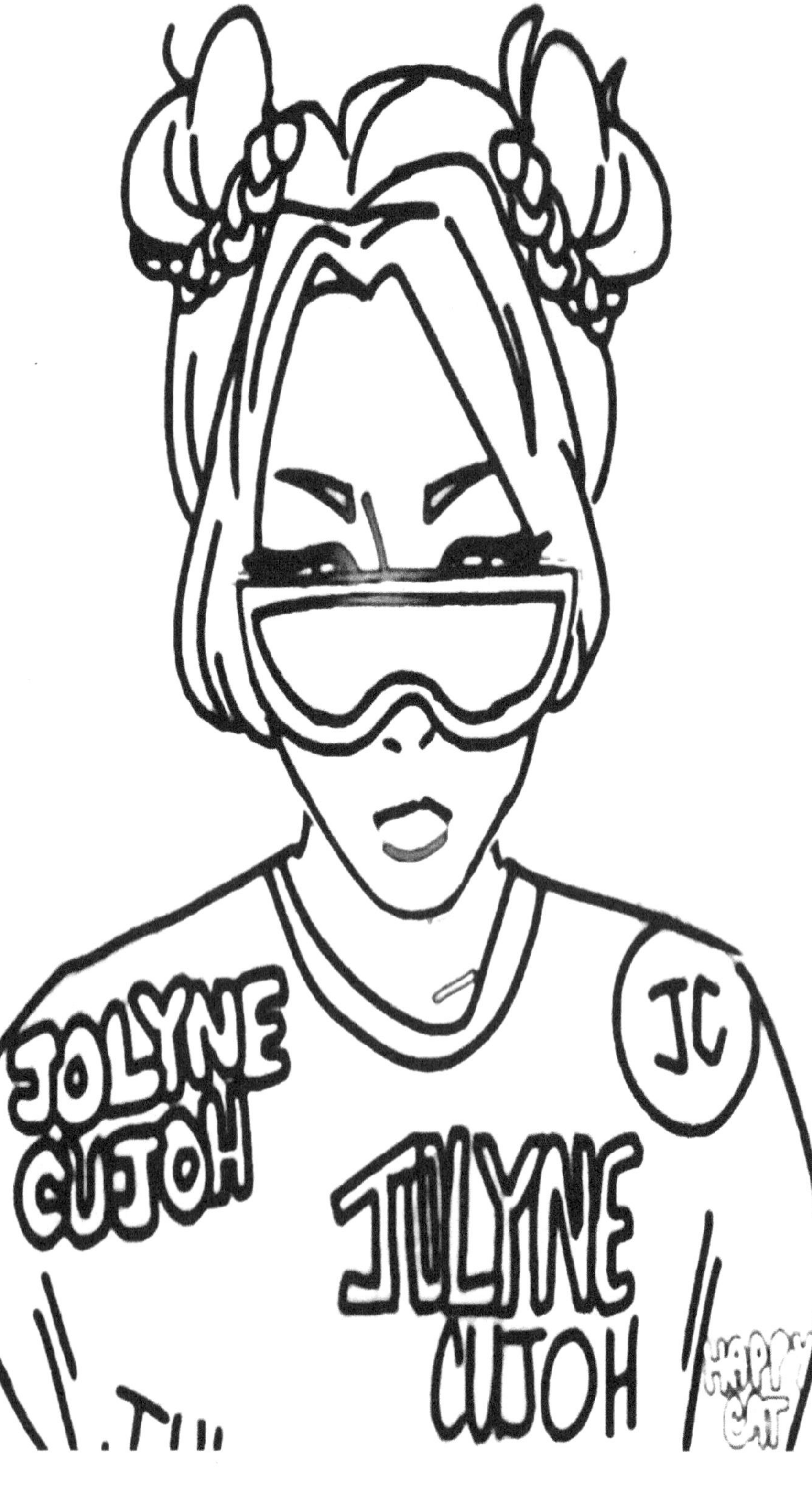
JOLYNE
CUJOH
JC
JOLYNE
CUJOH

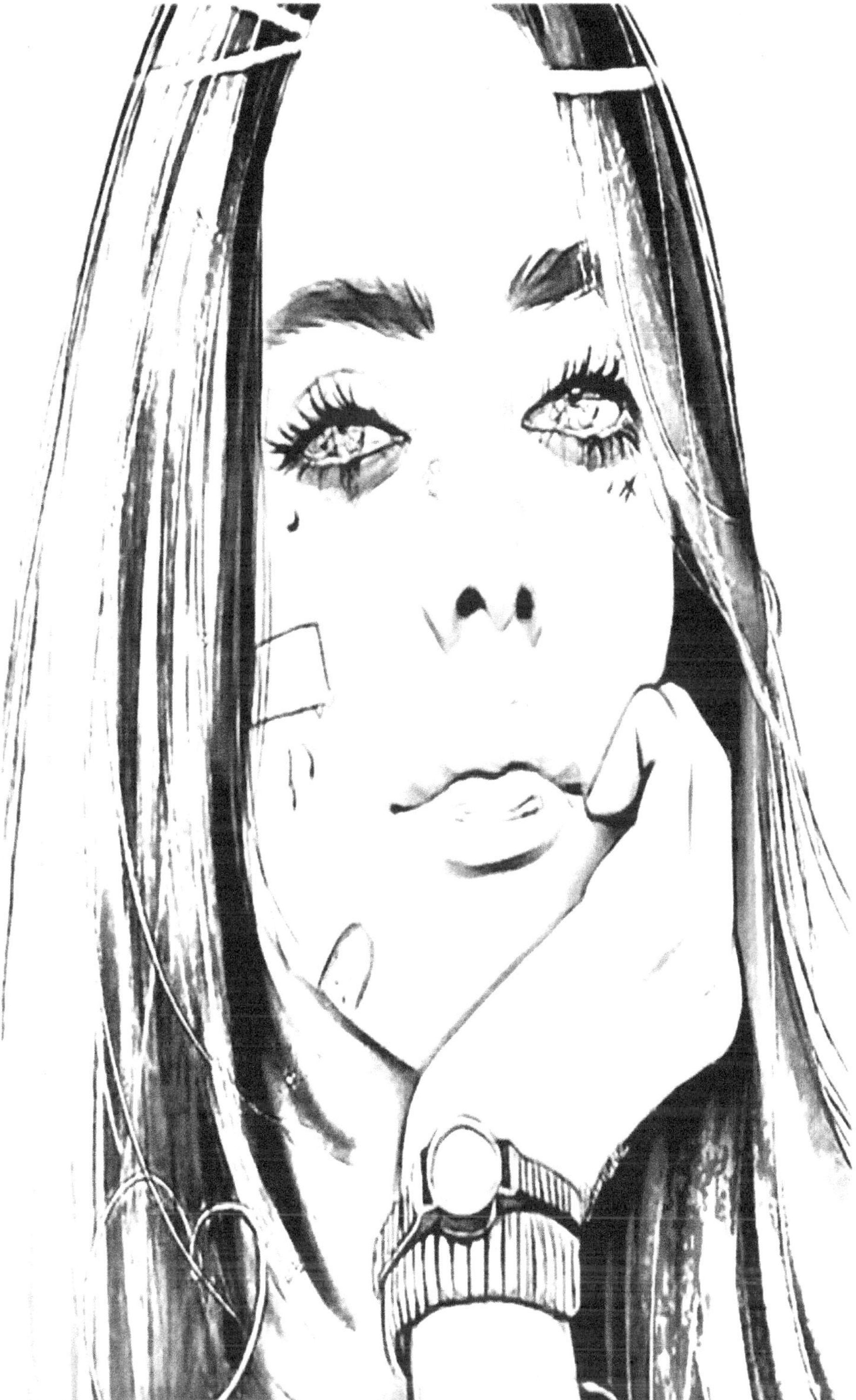

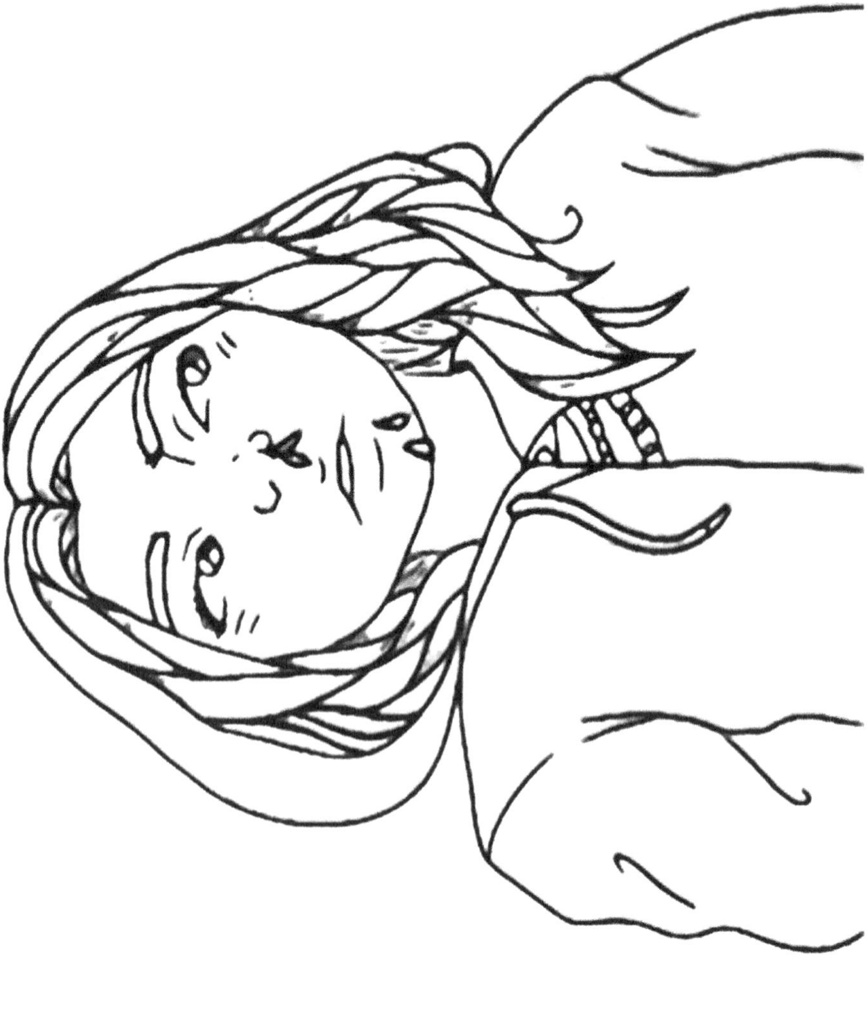

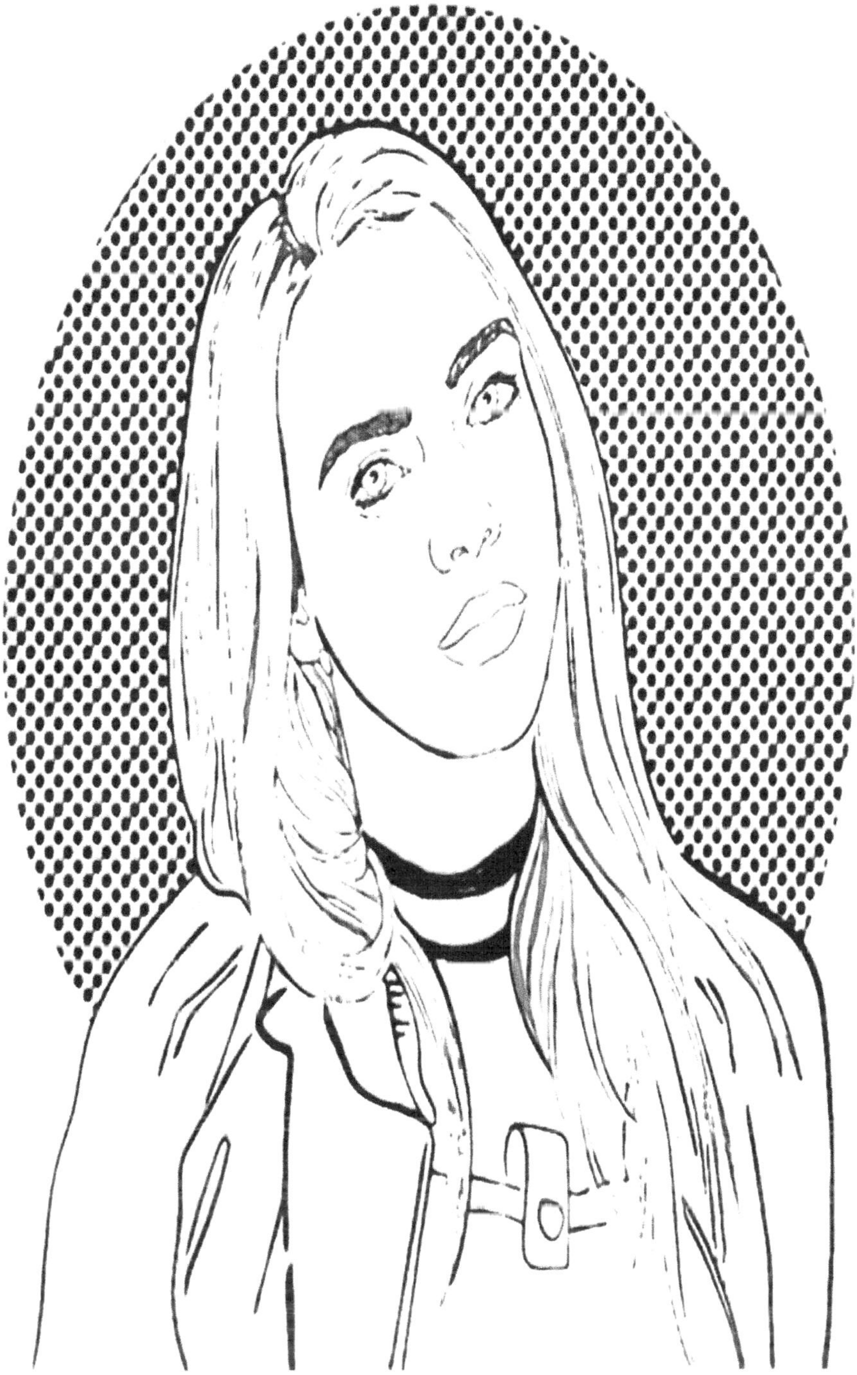

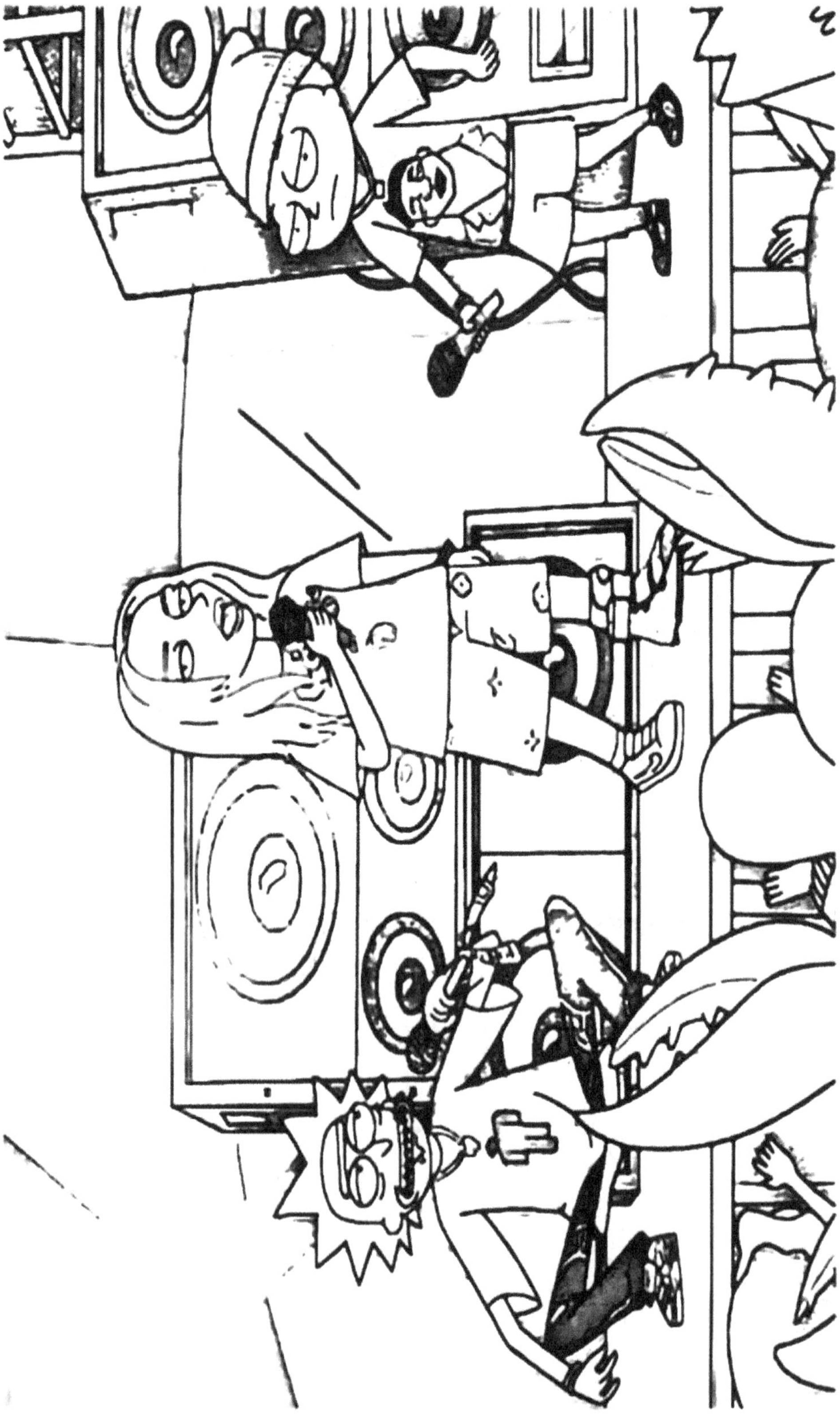

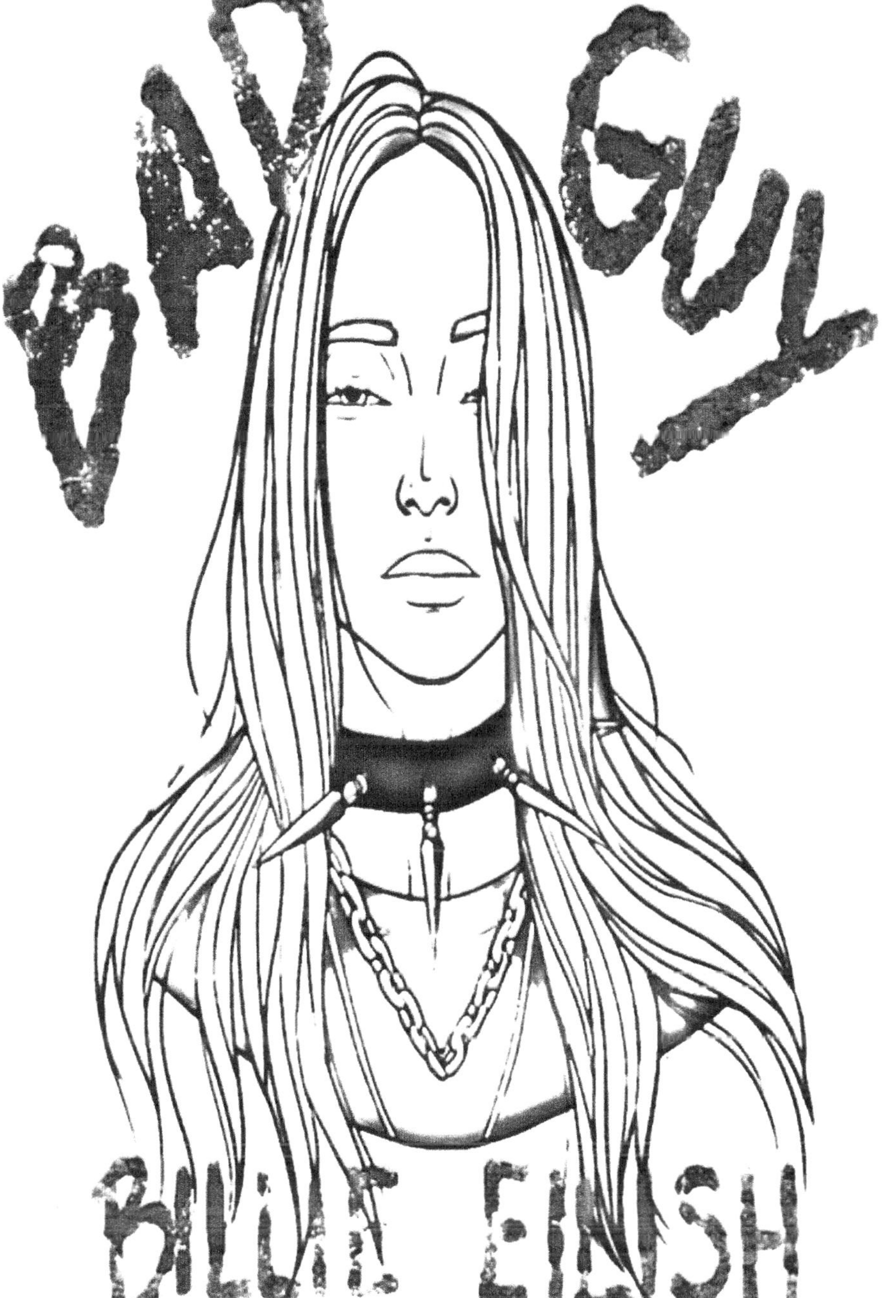
BAD GUY
BILLIE EILISH

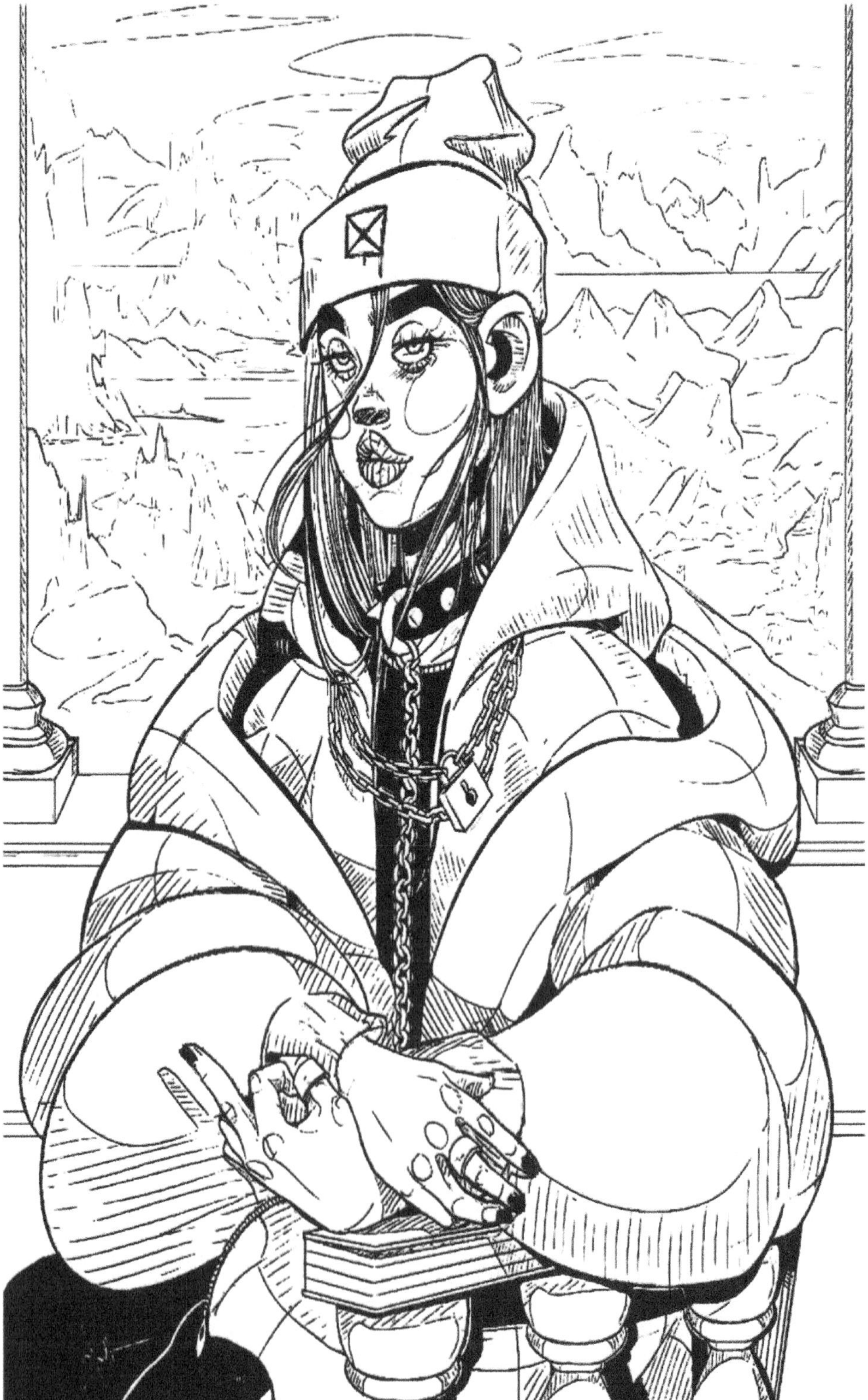

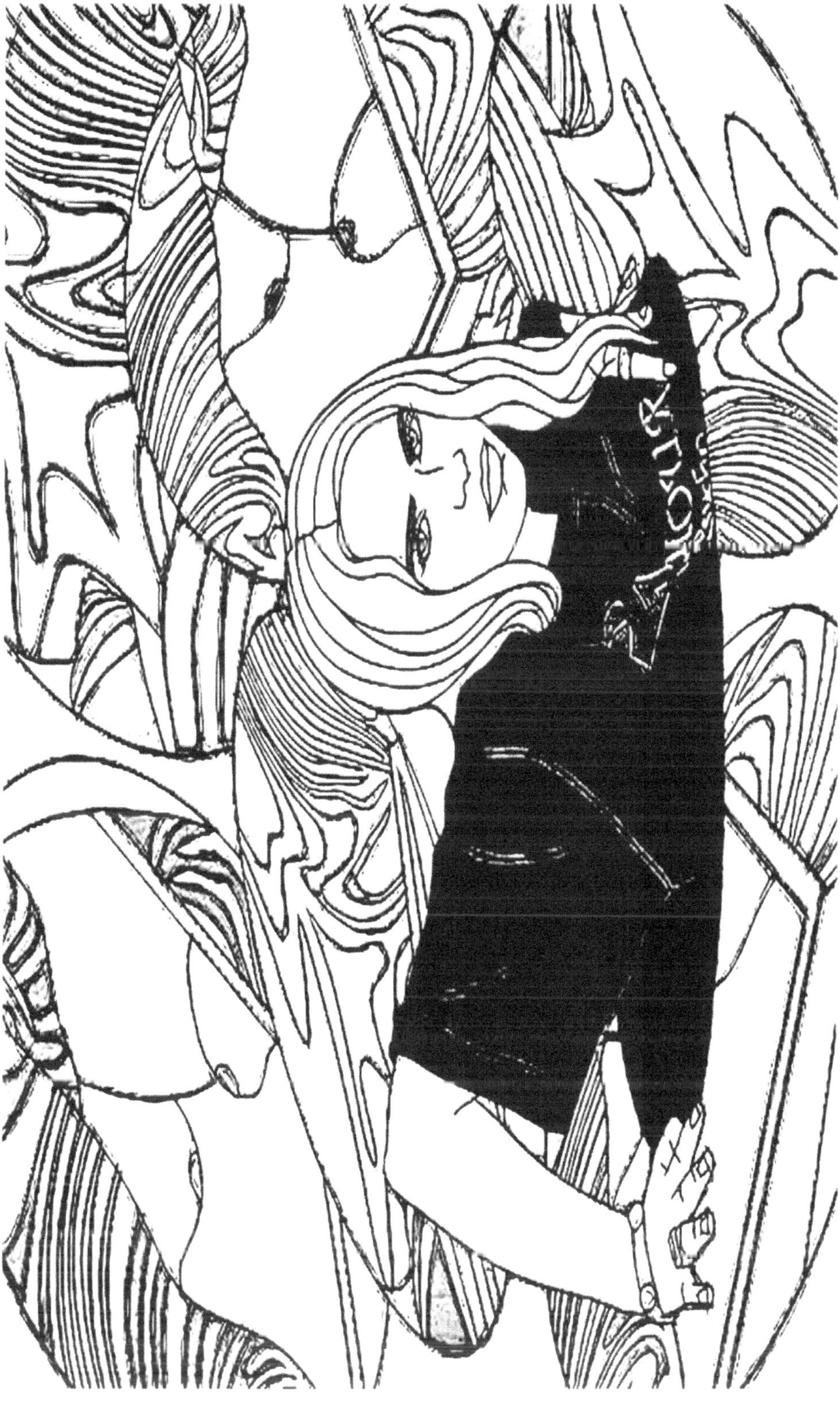

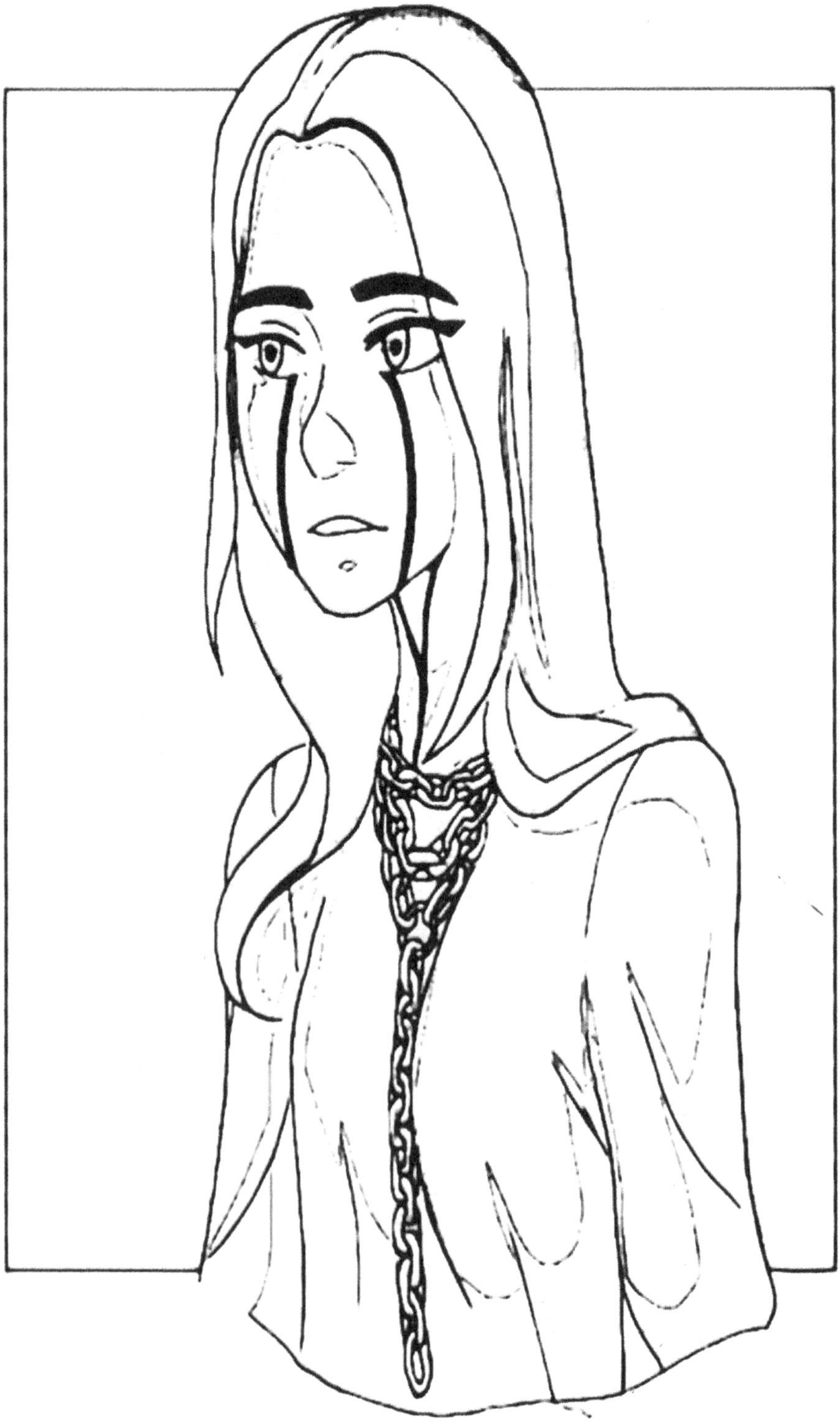

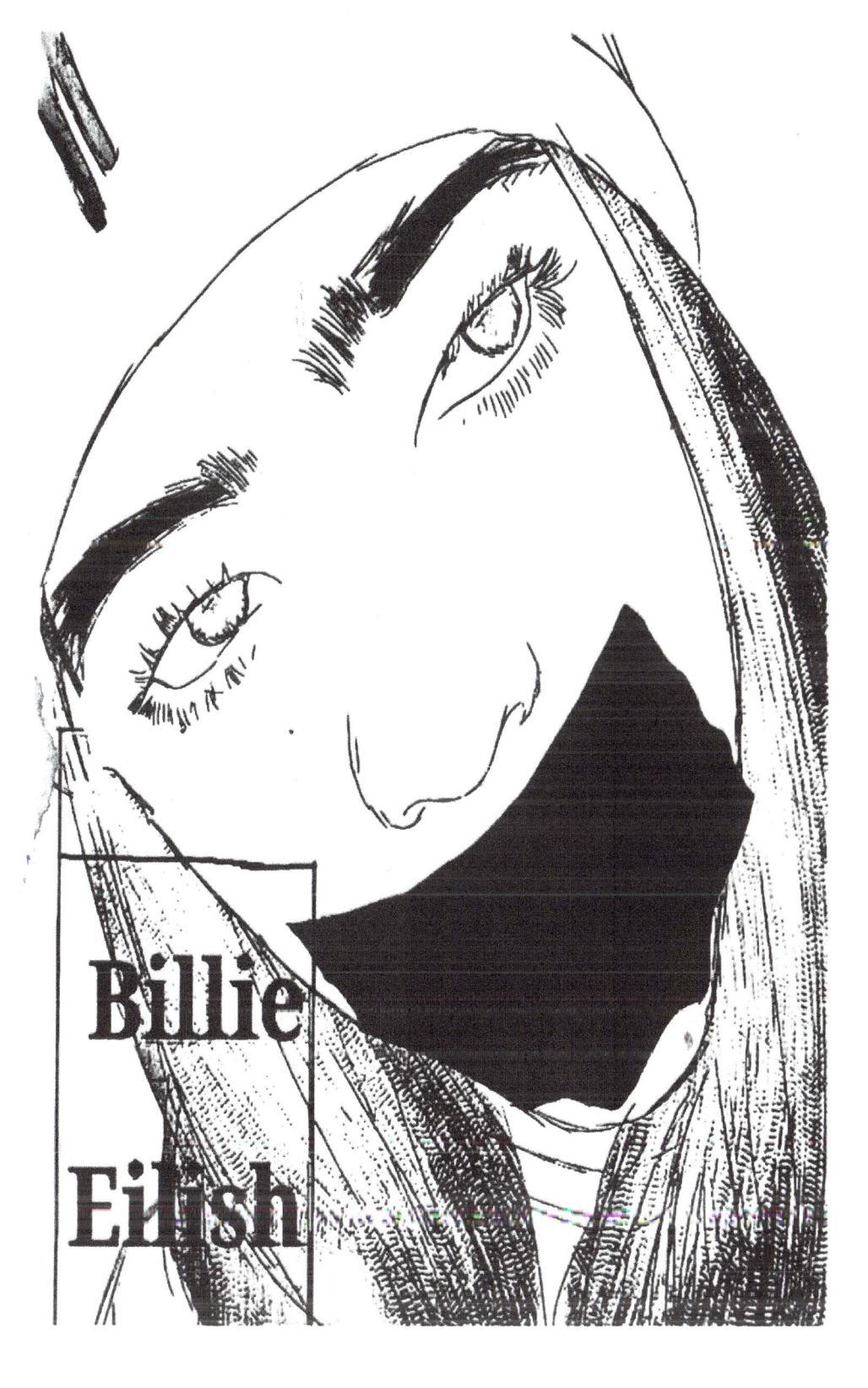

Billie Eilish

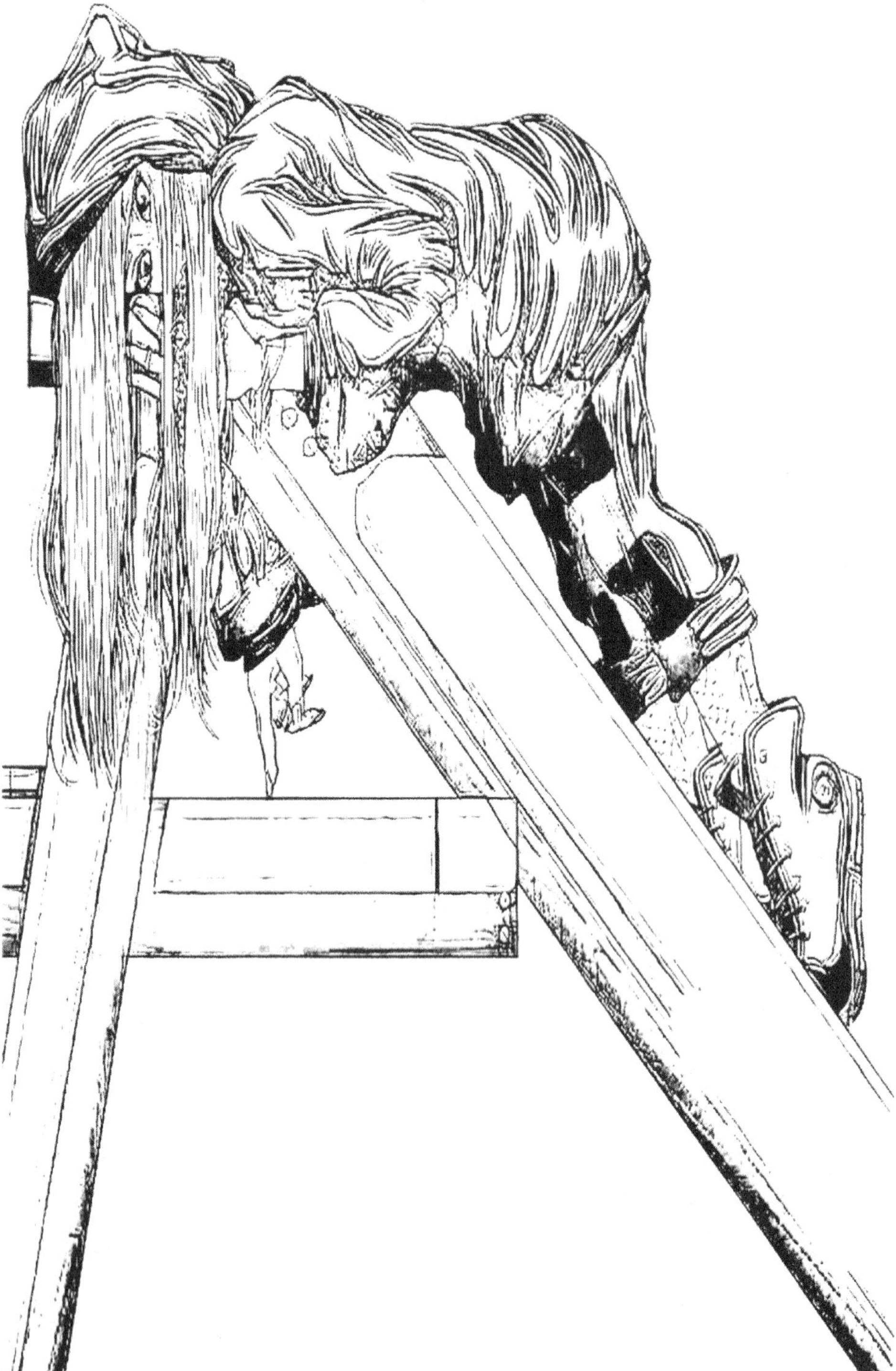

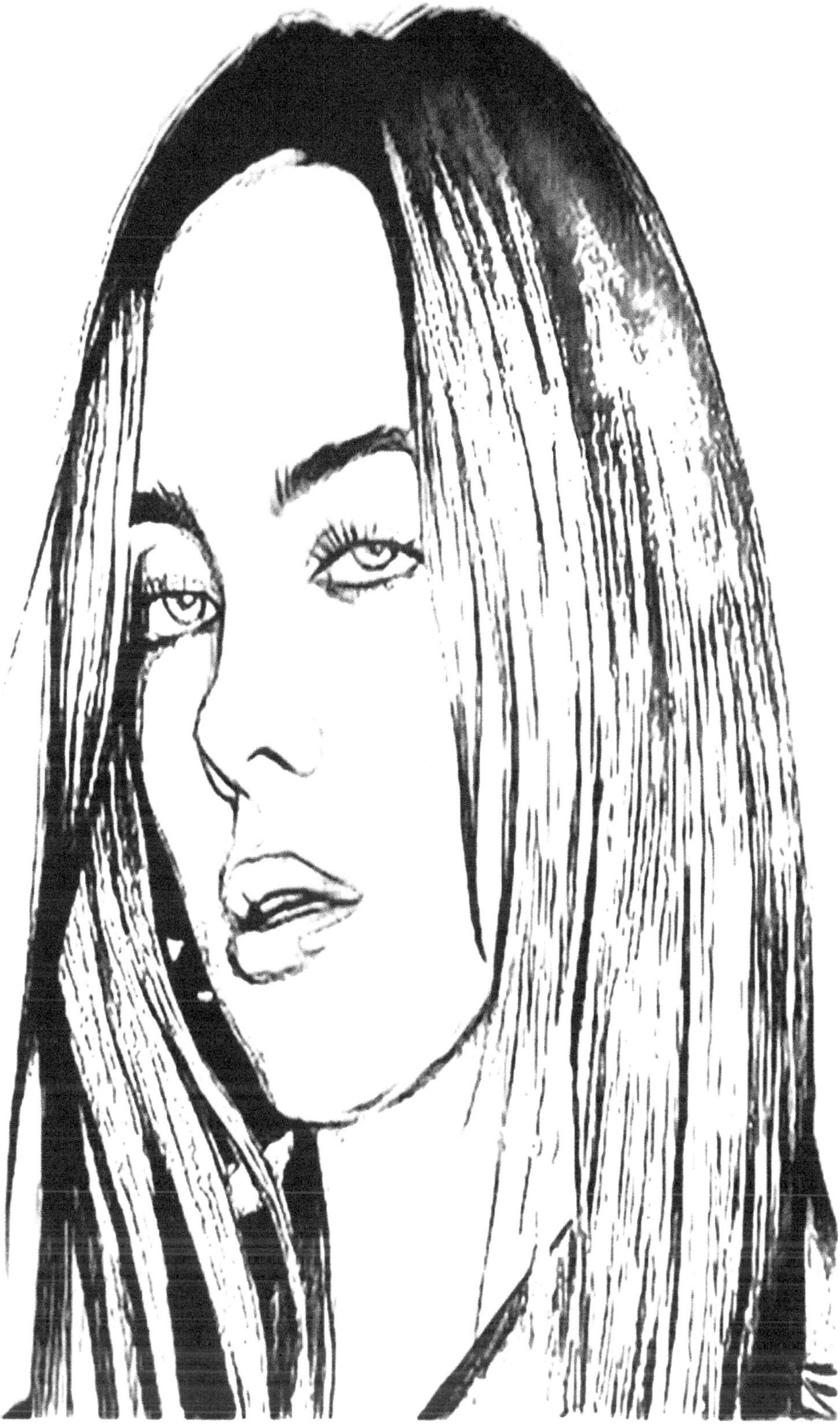

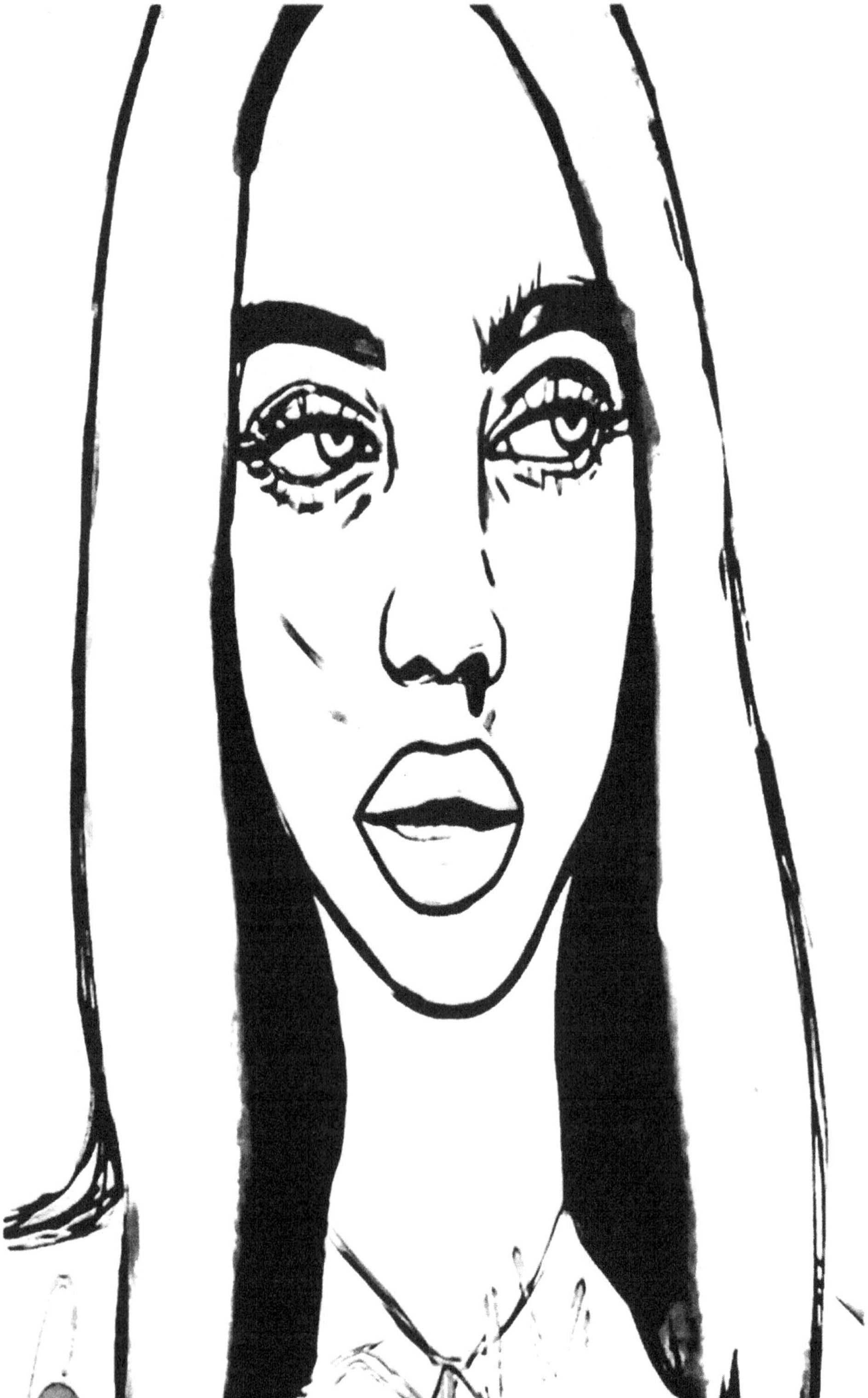

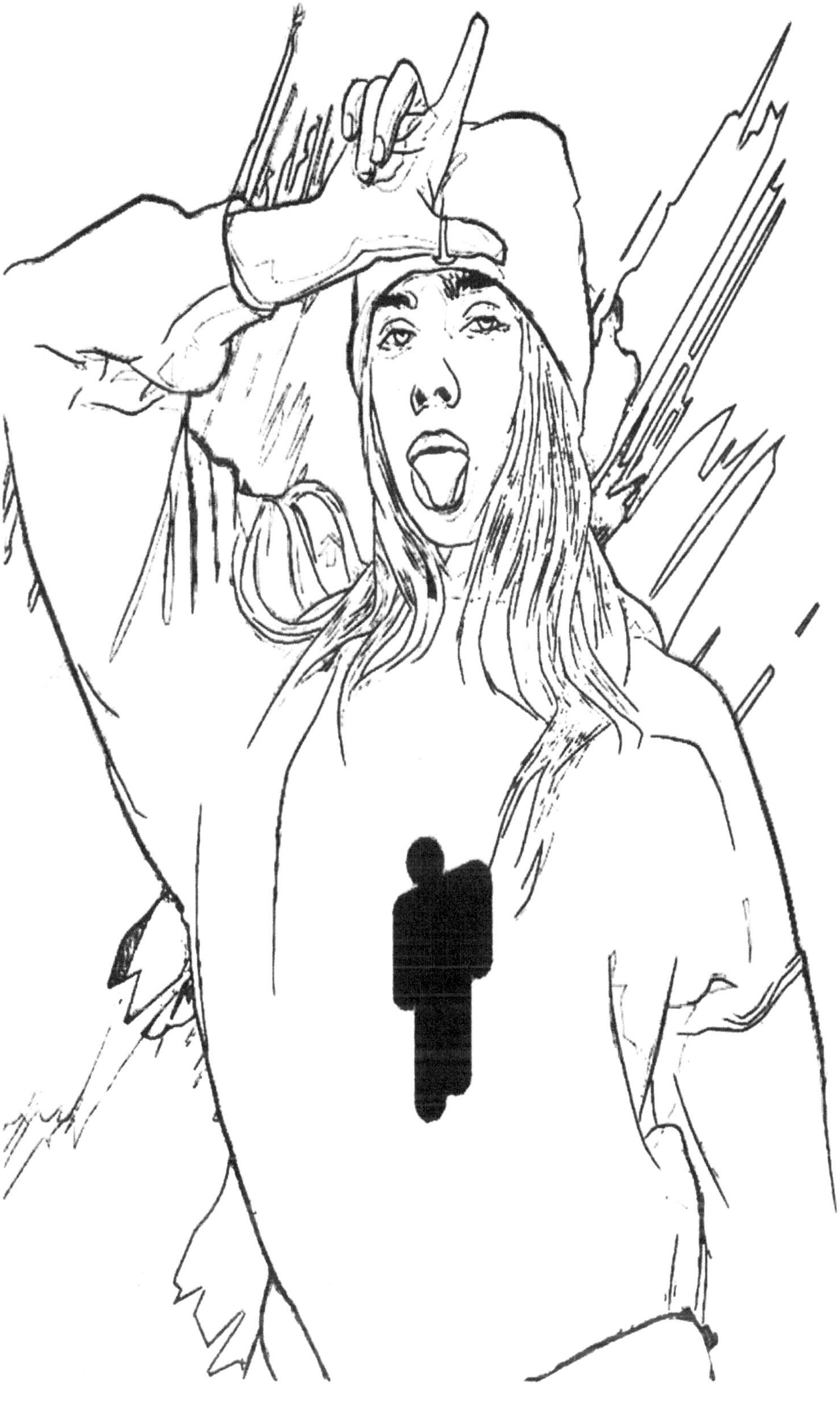

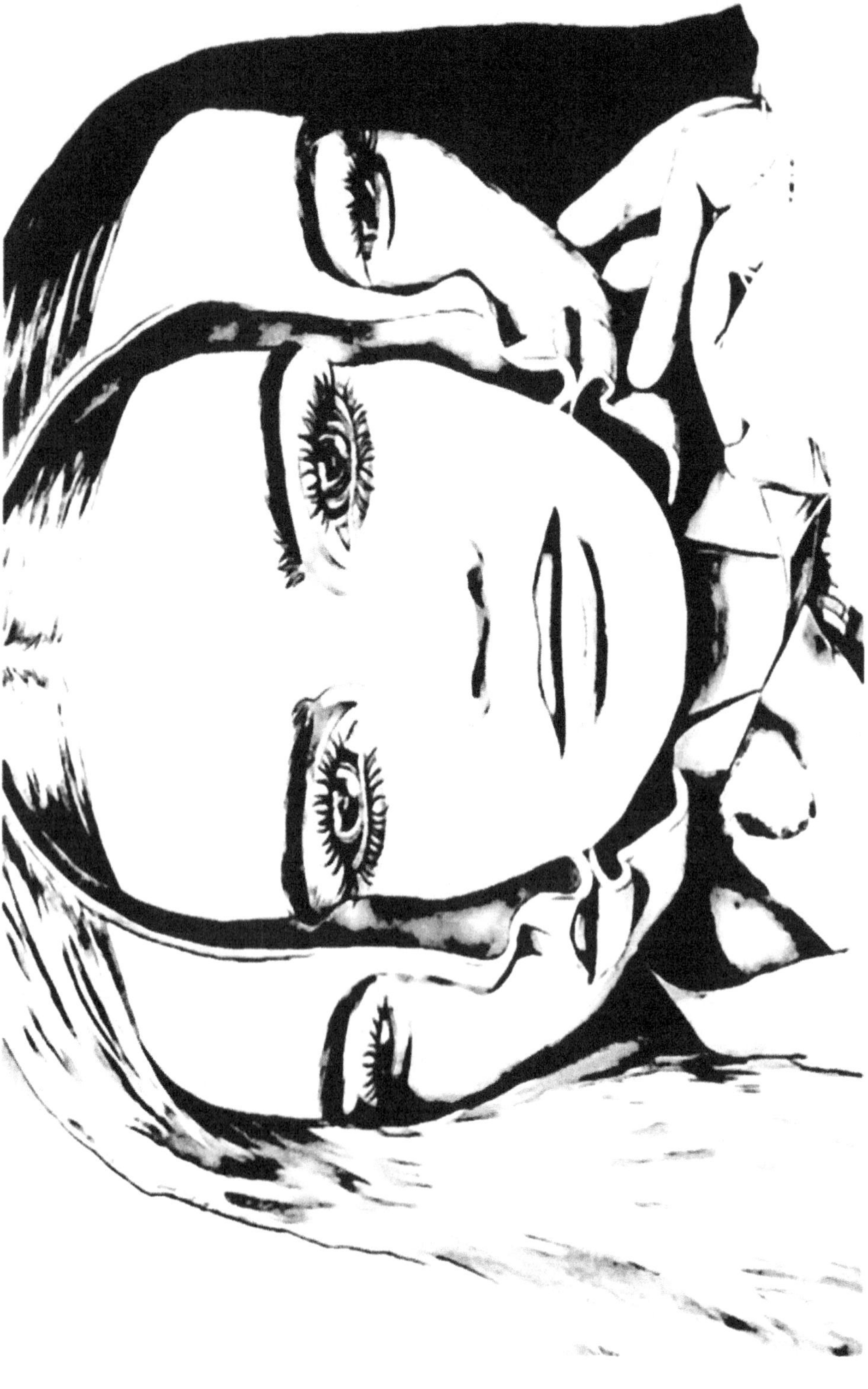

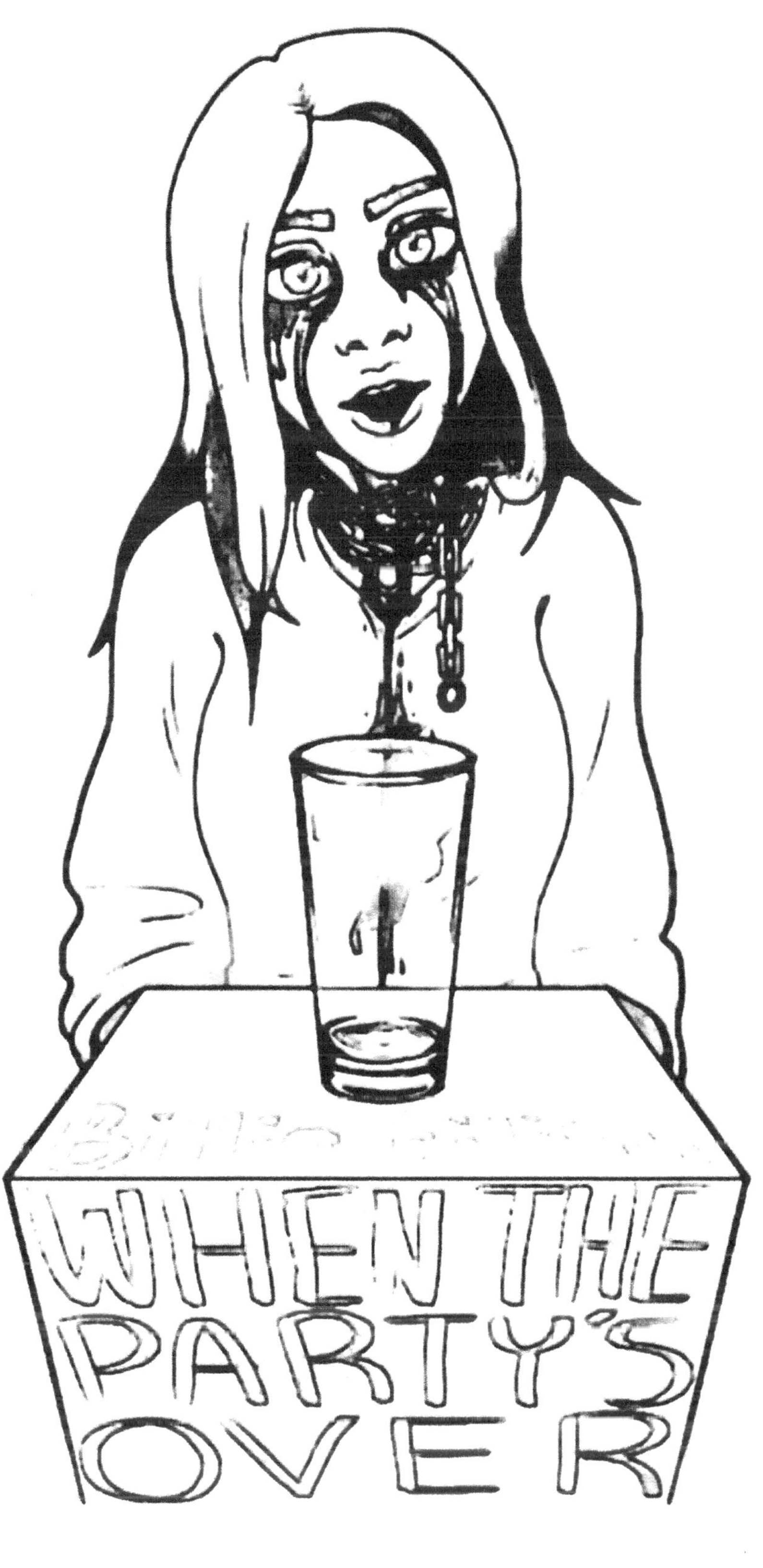
WHEN THE
PARTY'S
OVER

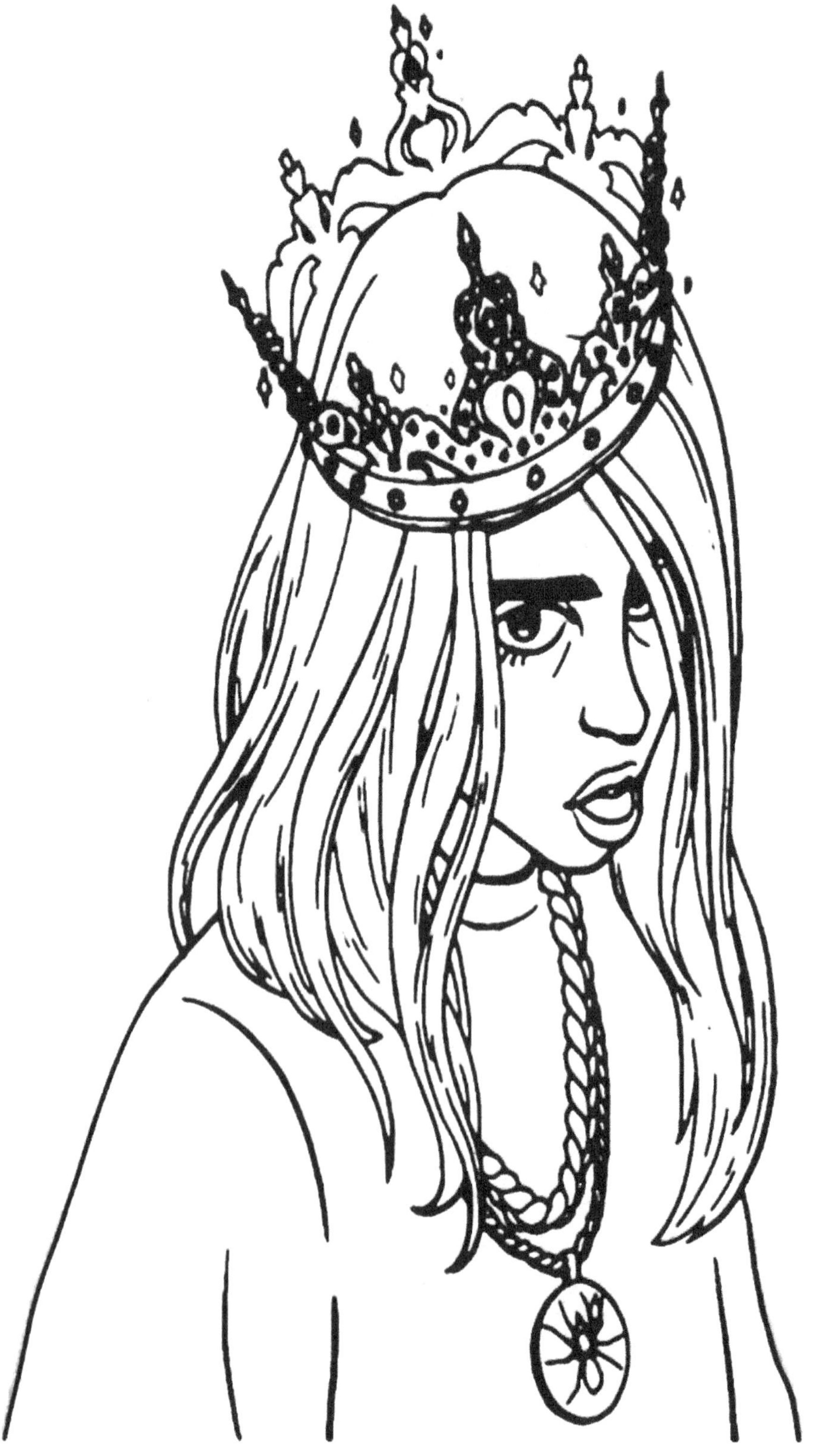

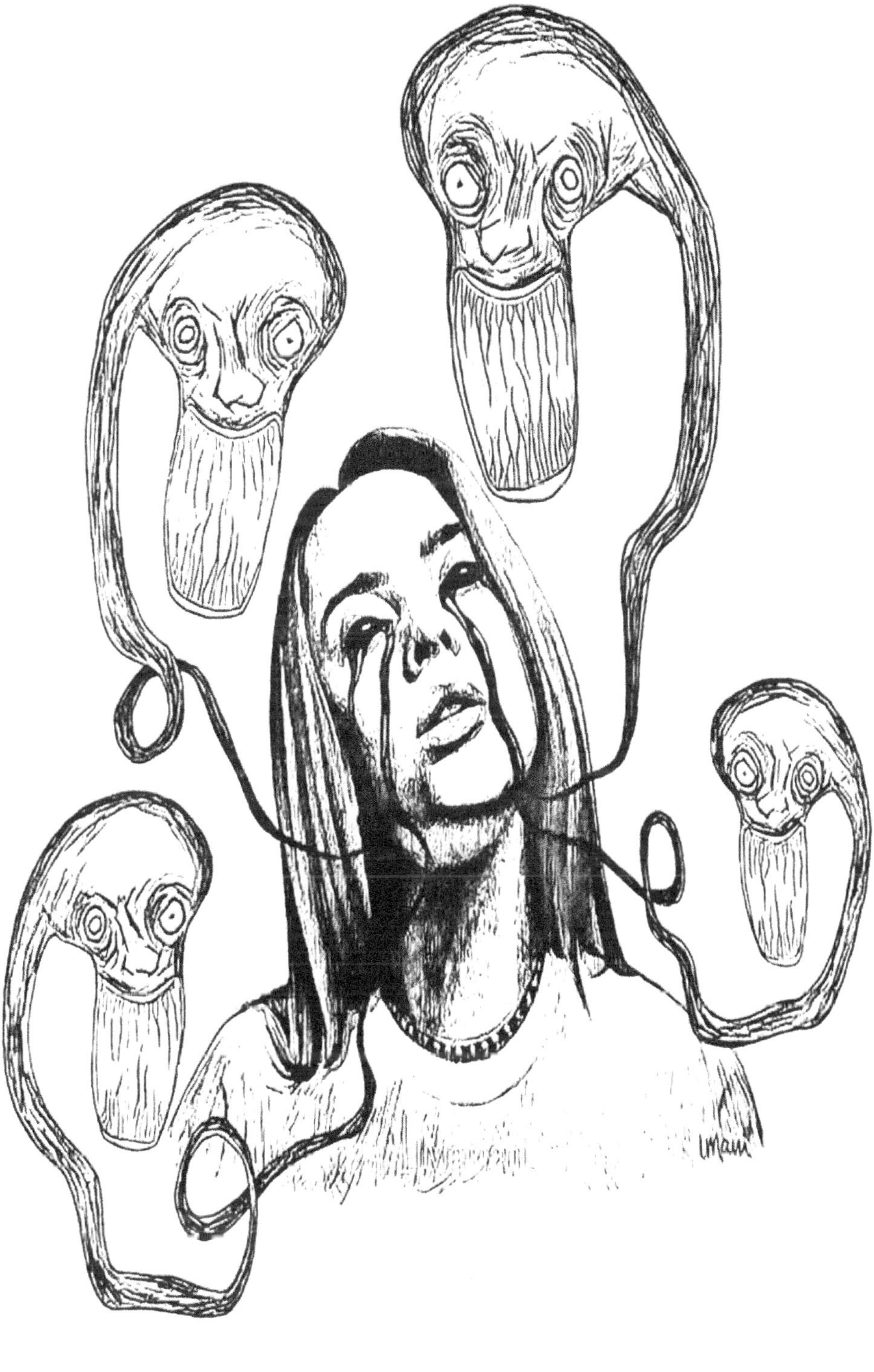

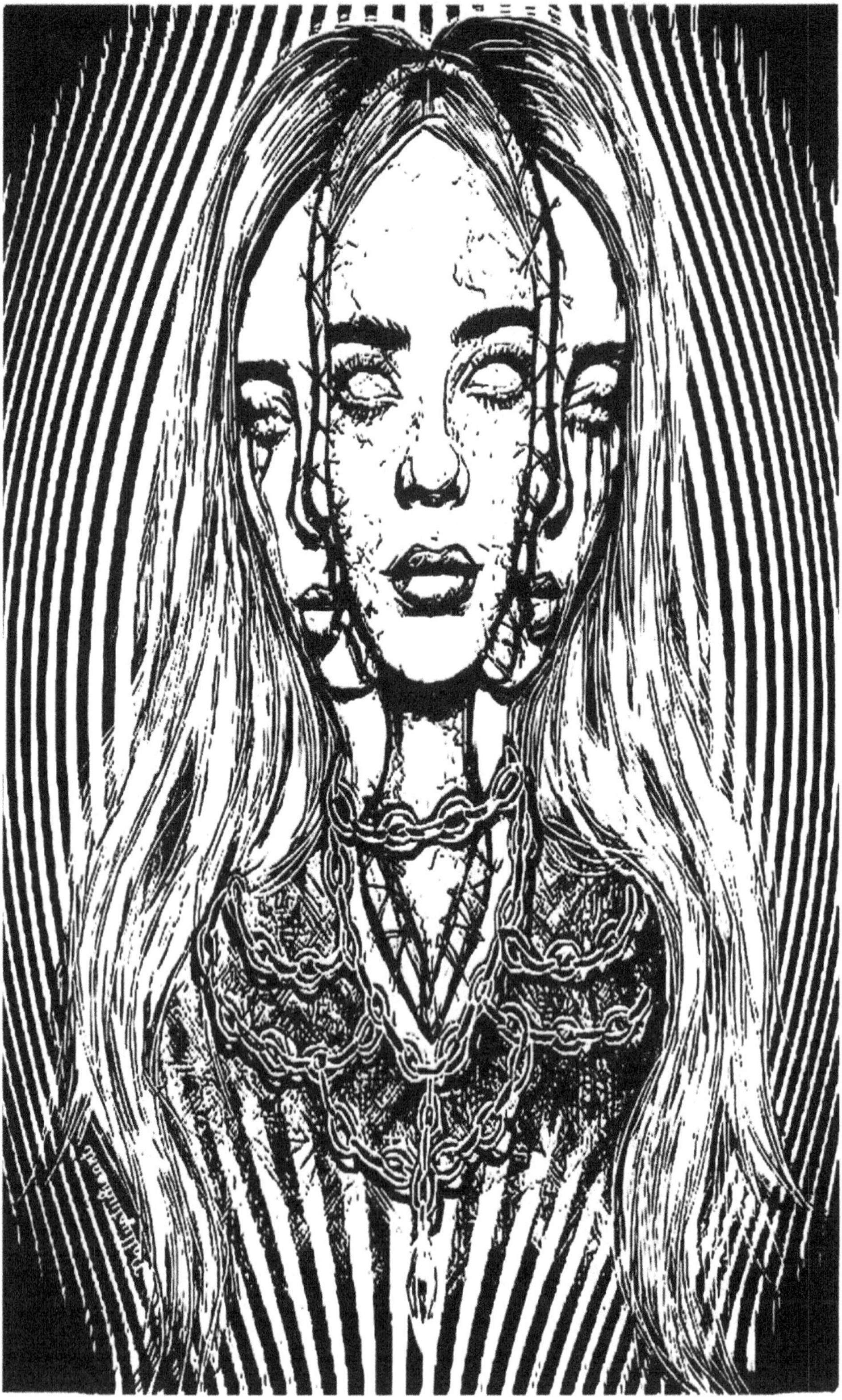

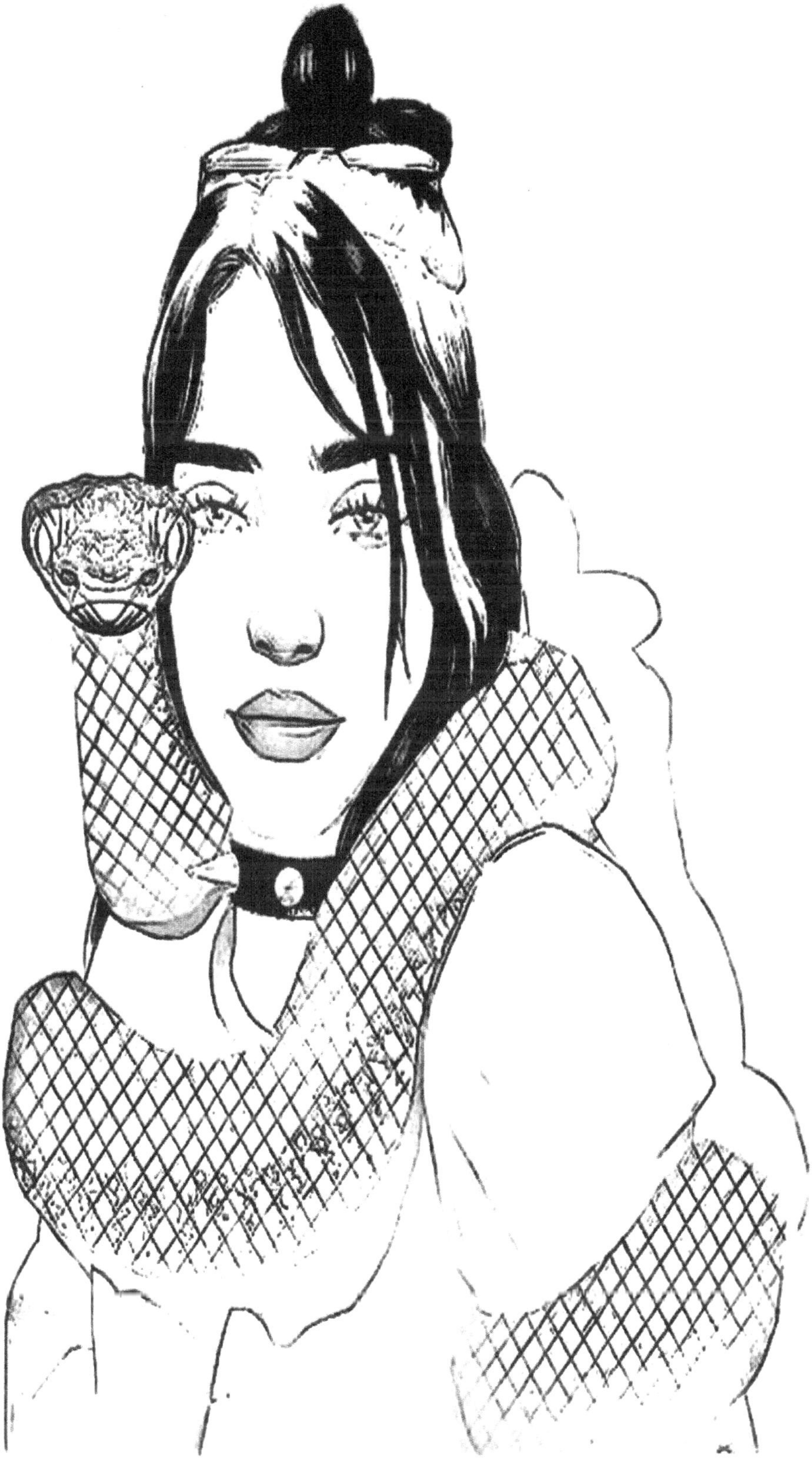

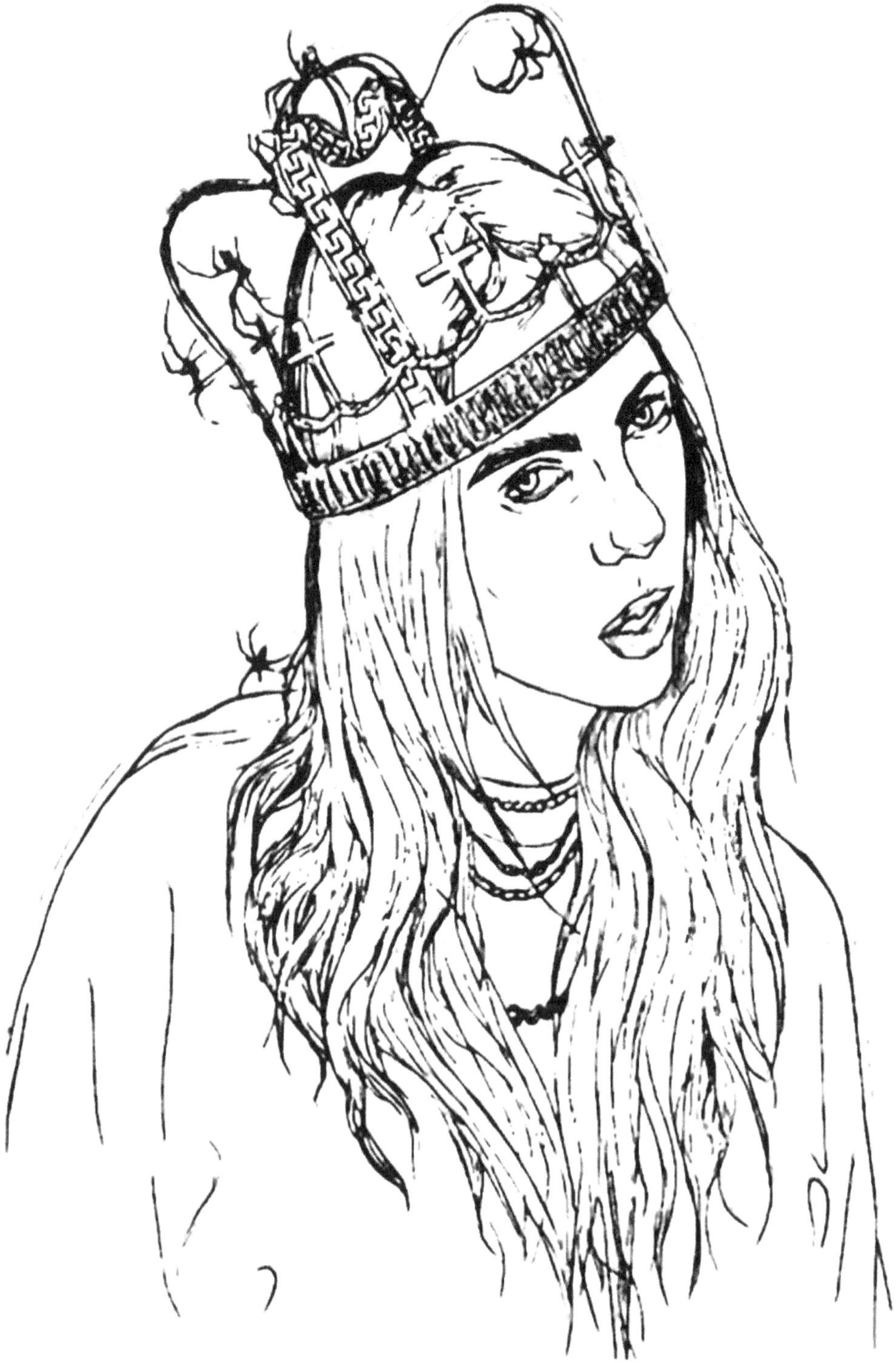

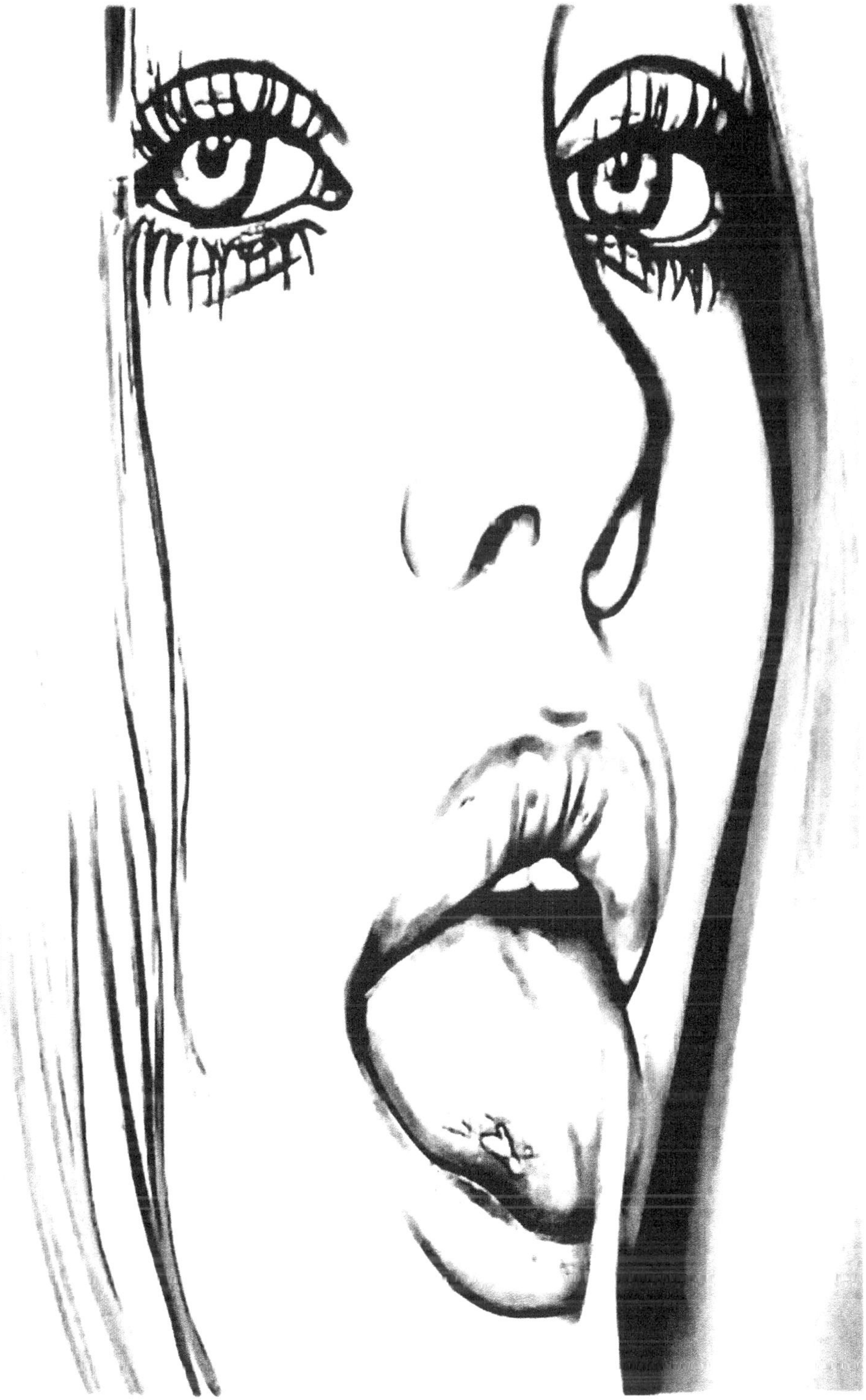

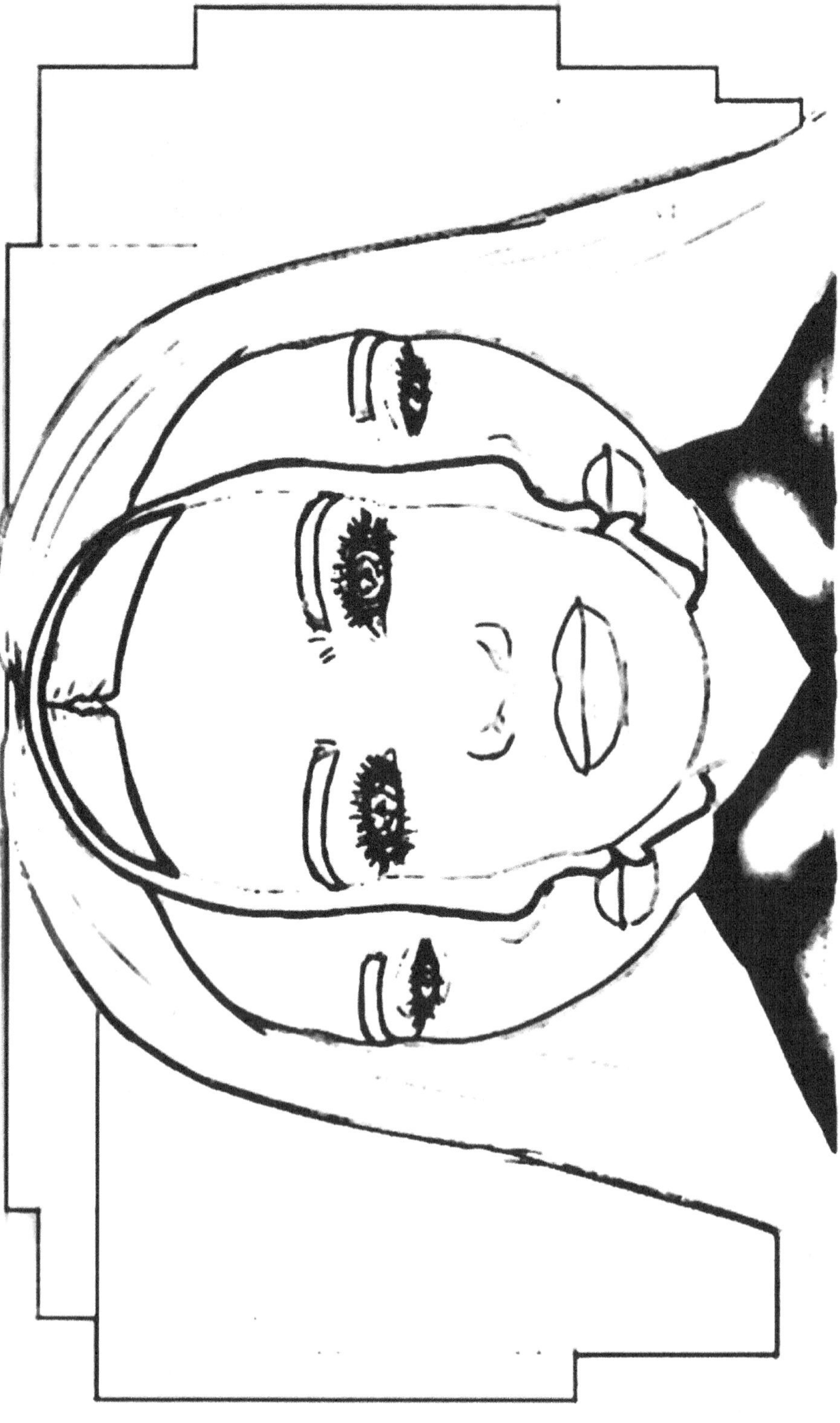

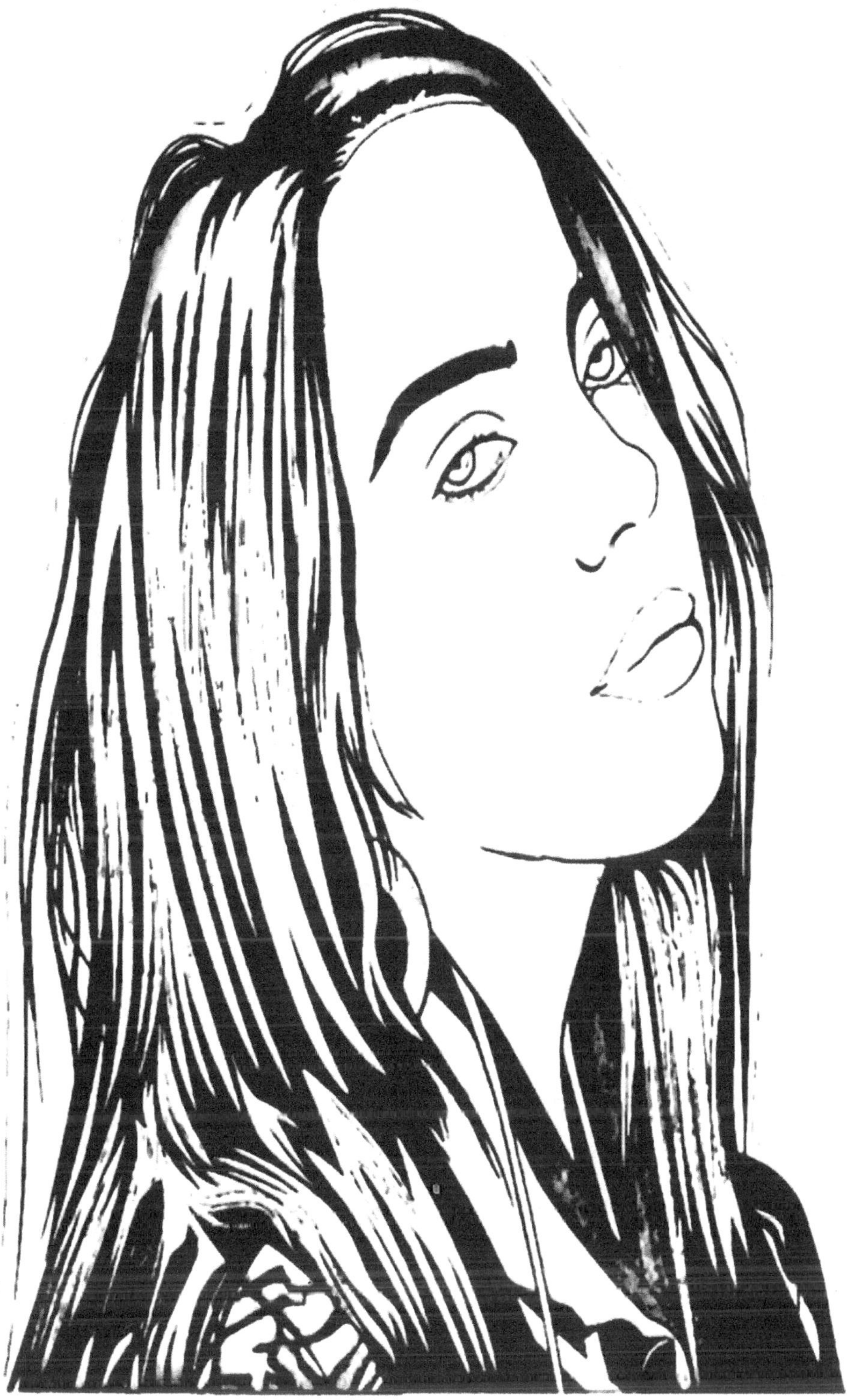

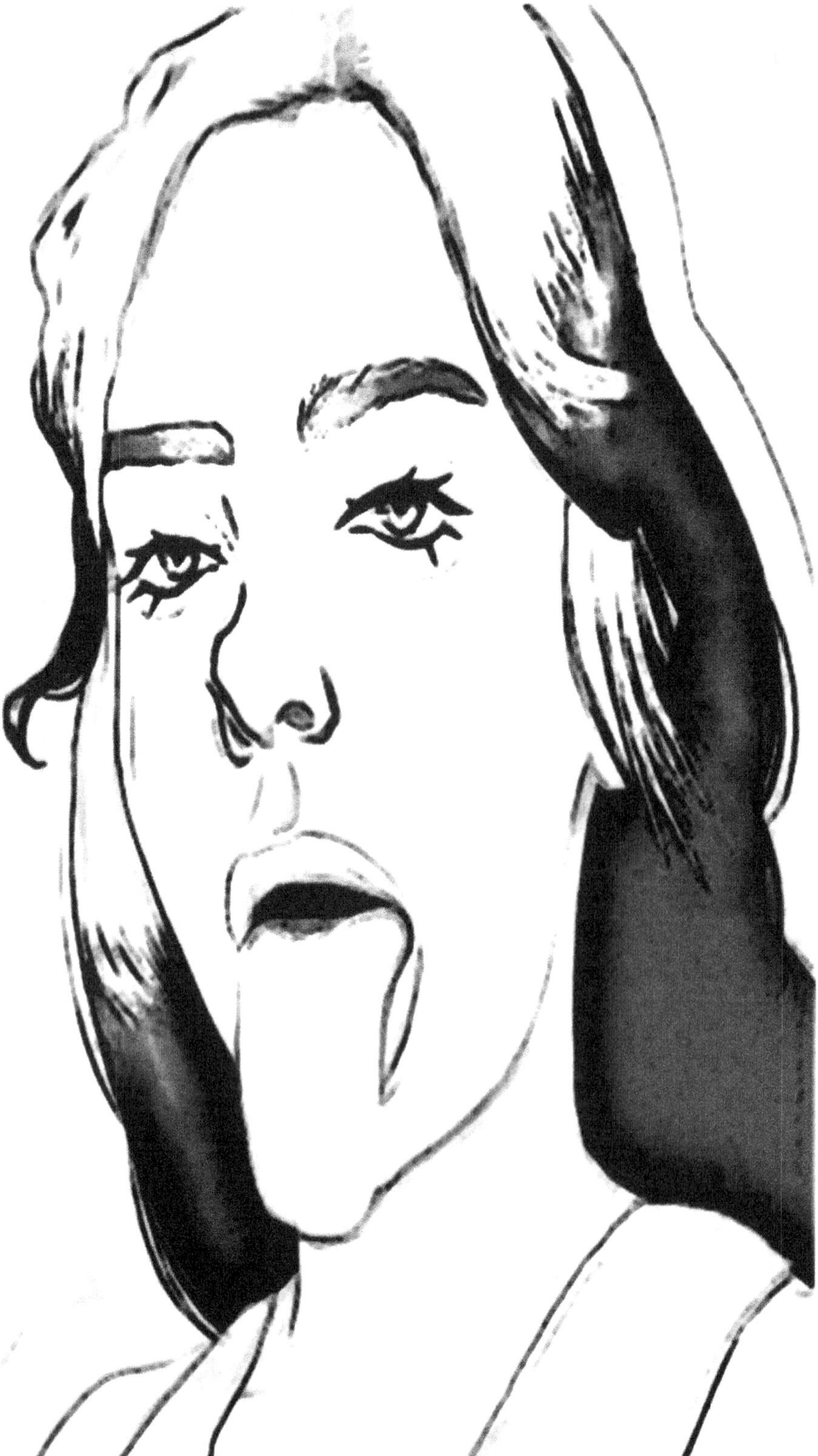

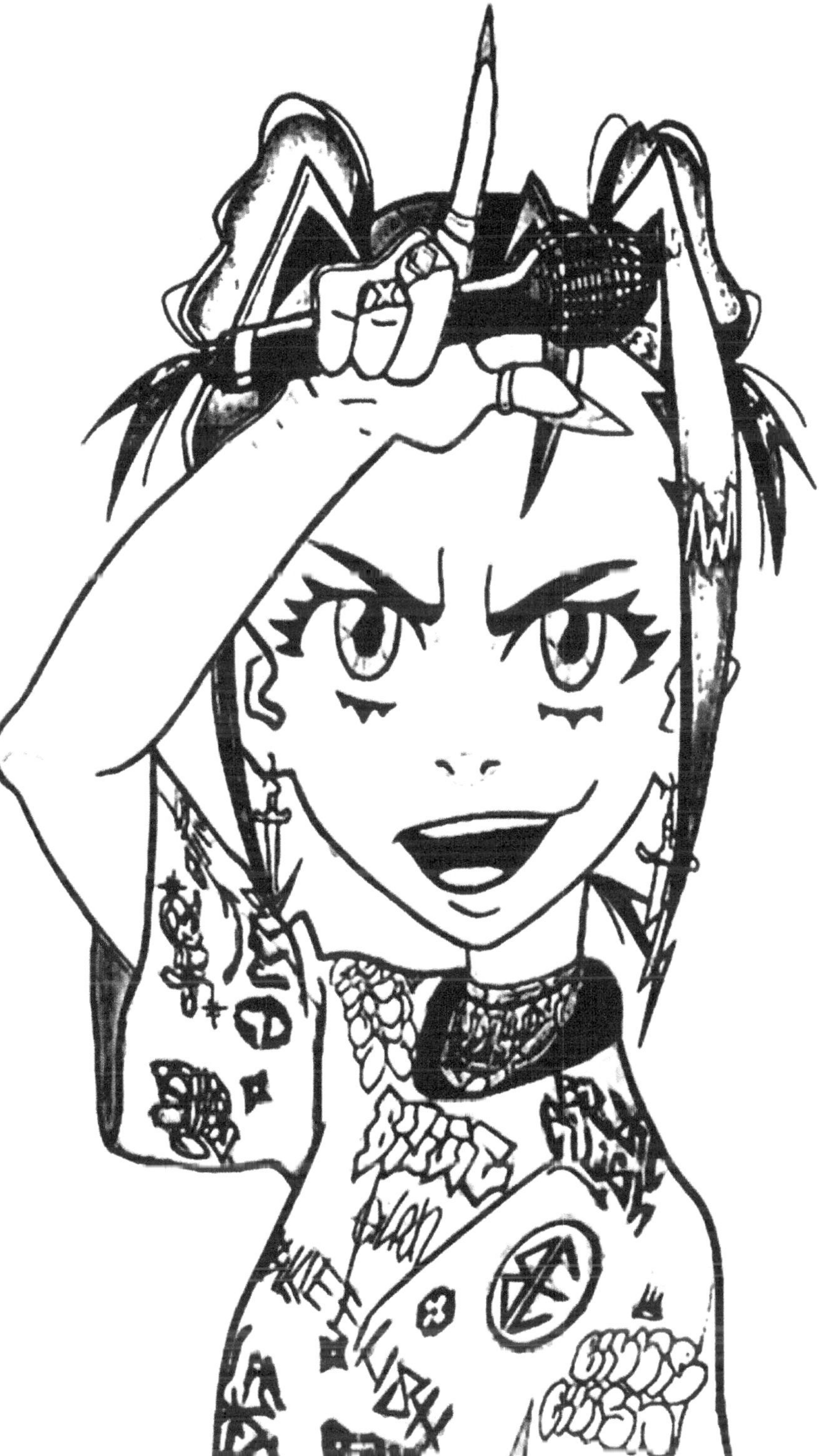

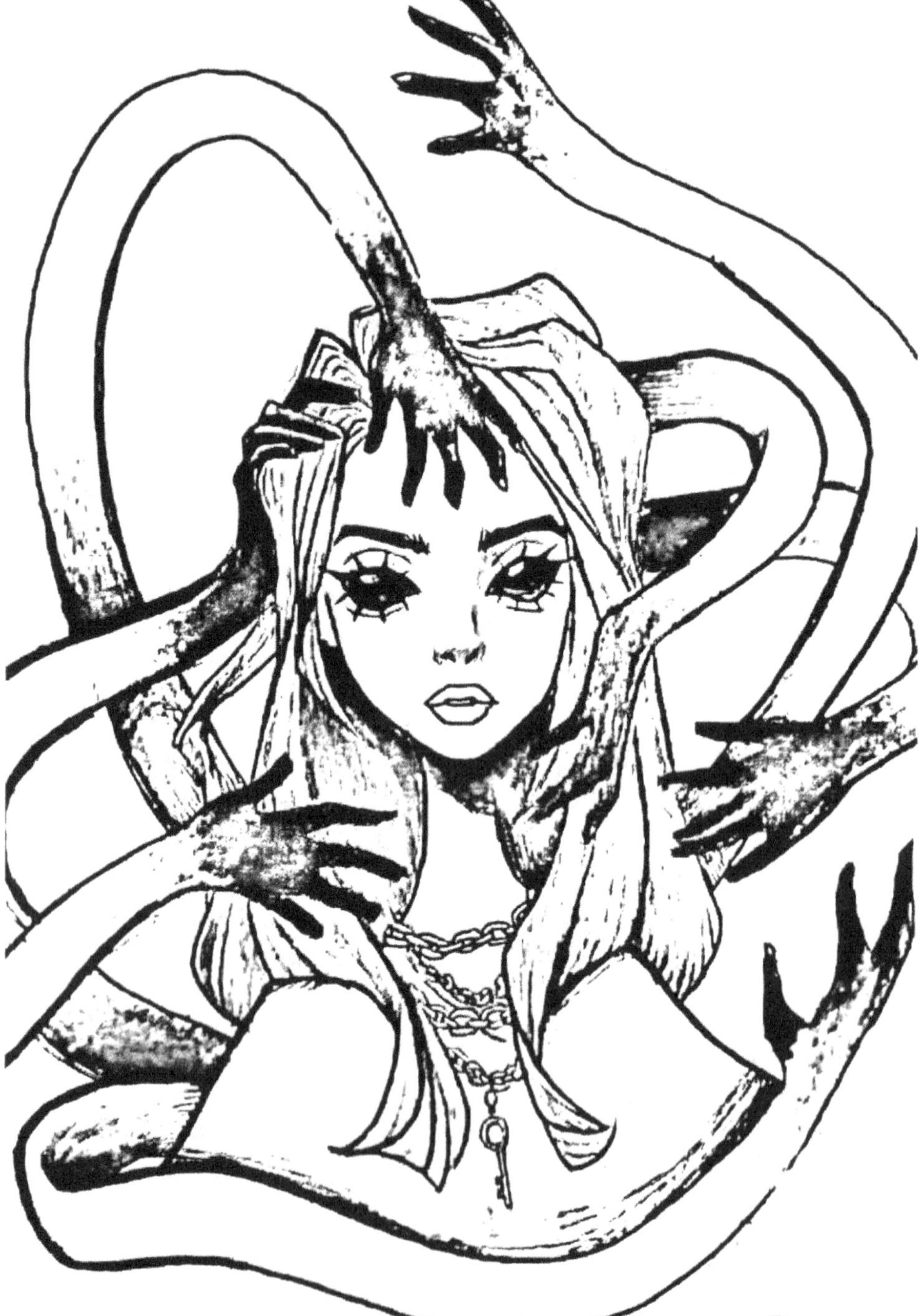

WHEN WE ALL FALL ASLEEP,
WHERE D@ WE GO?

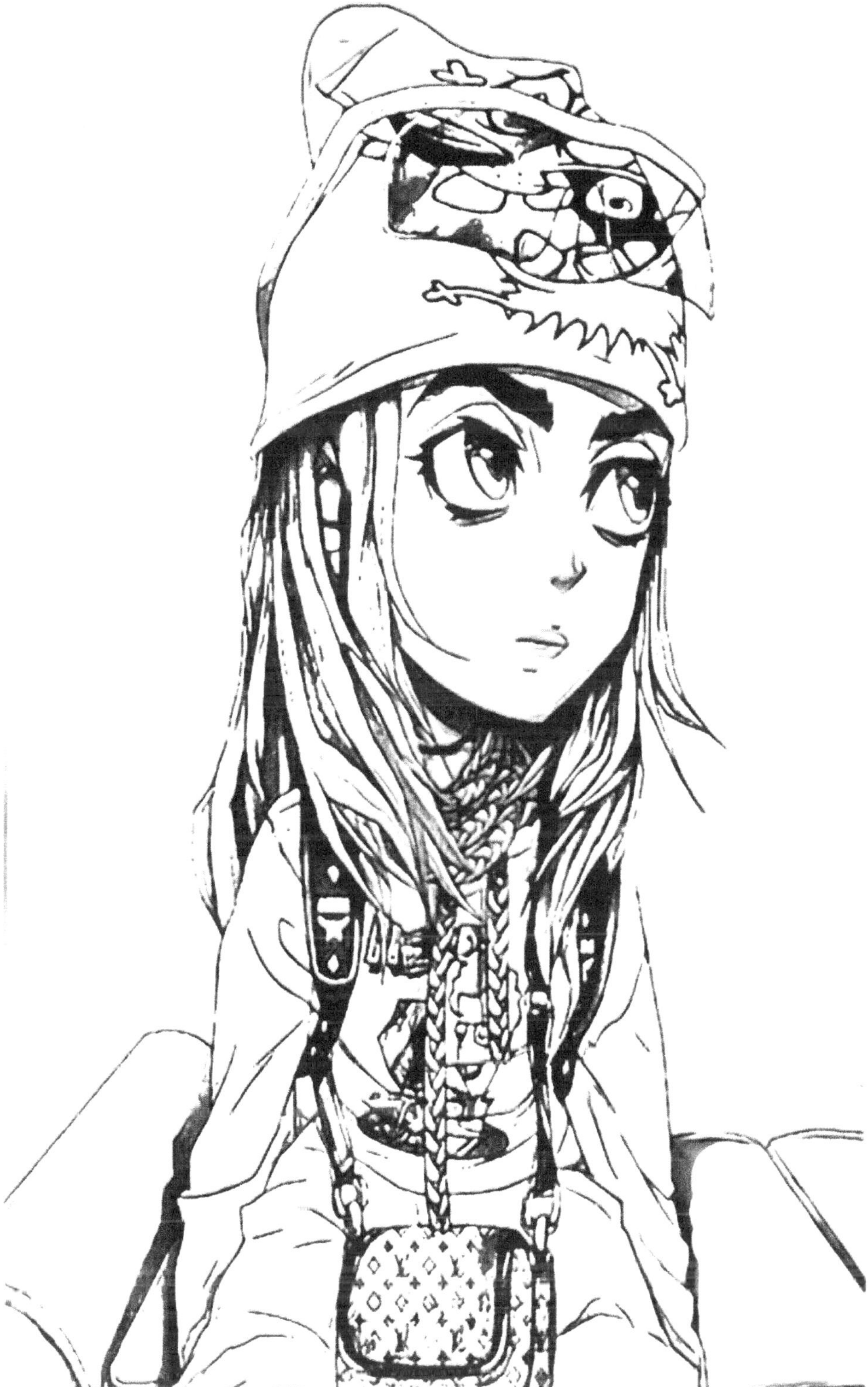

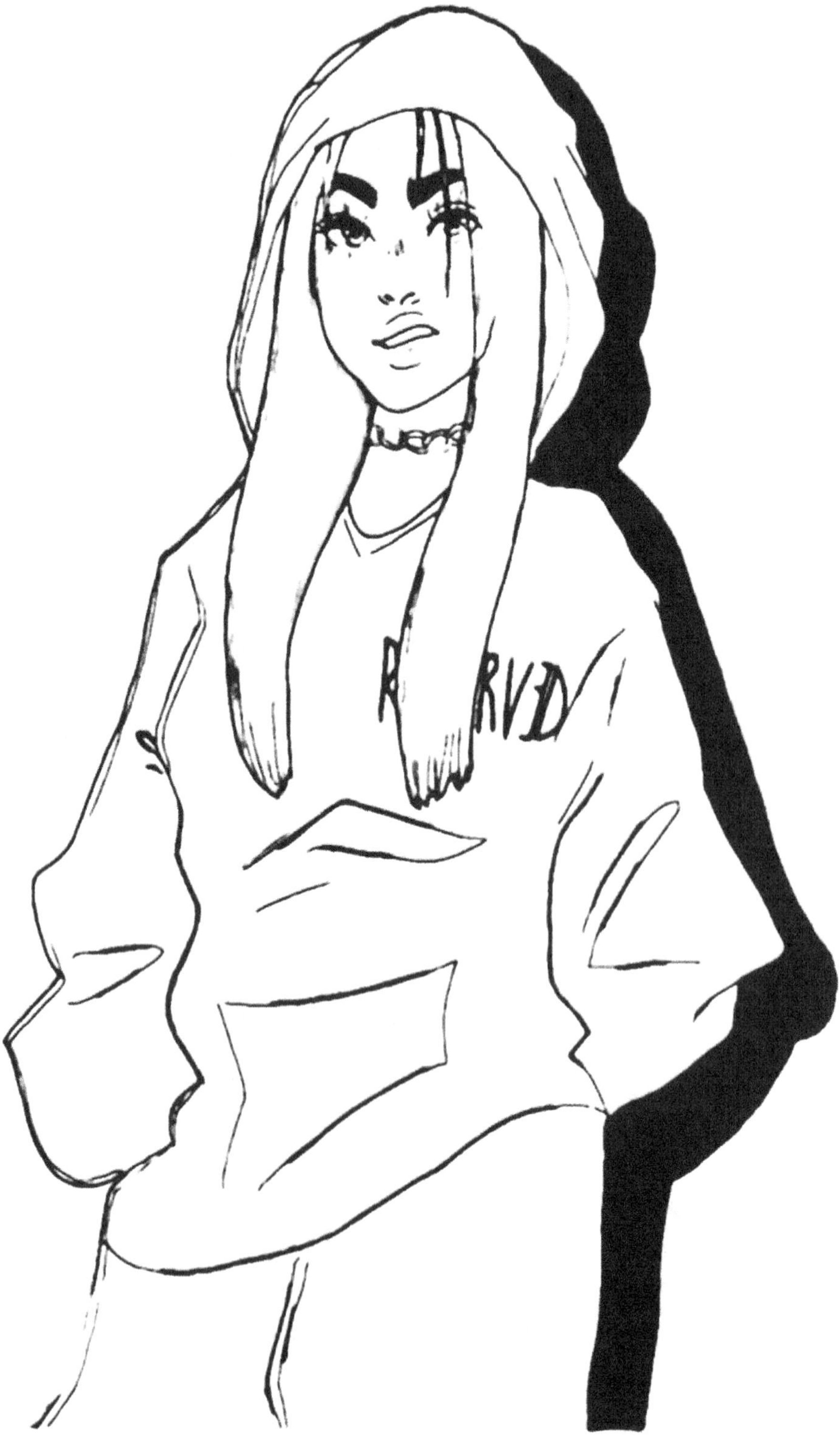

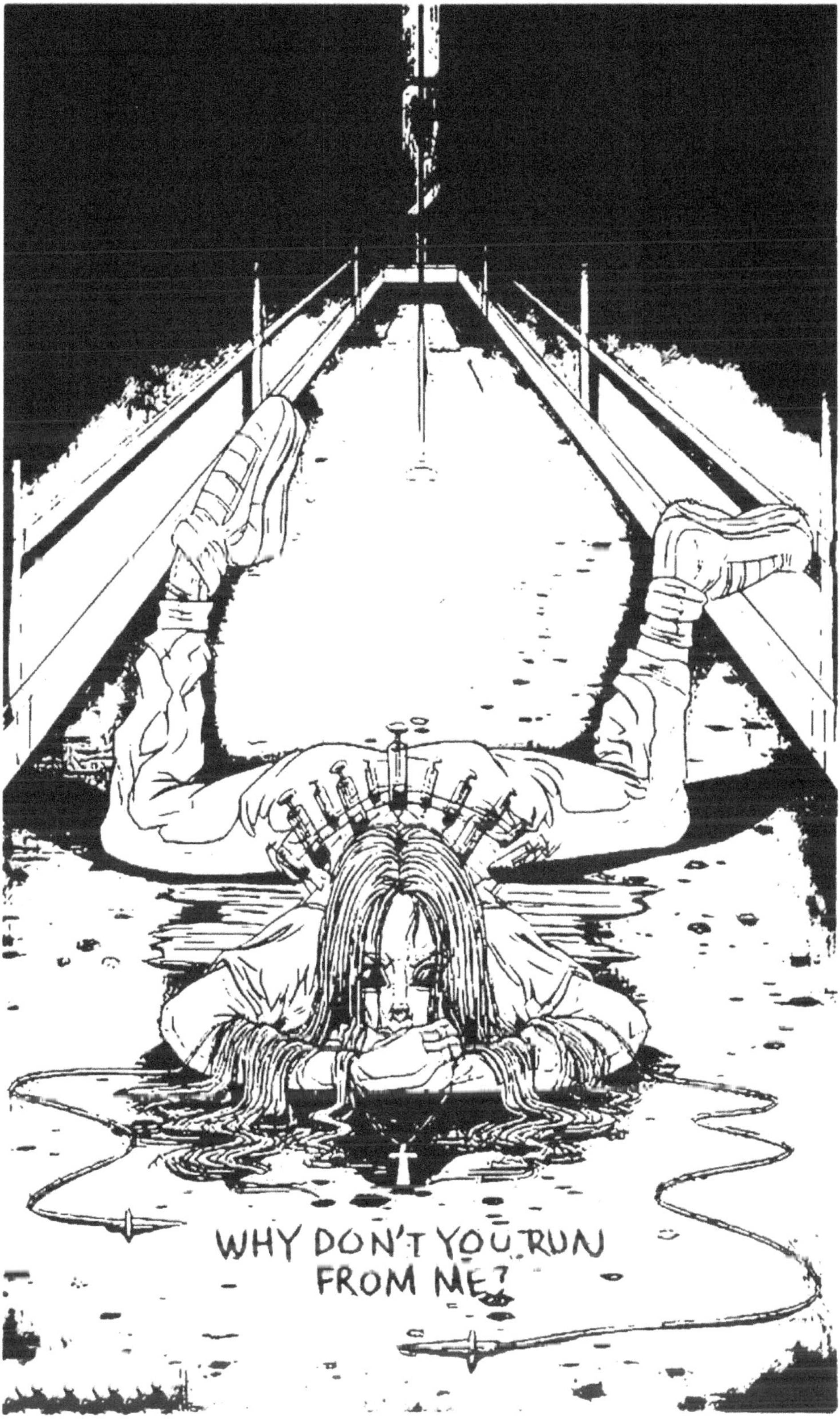
WHY DON'T YOU RUN
FROM ME?

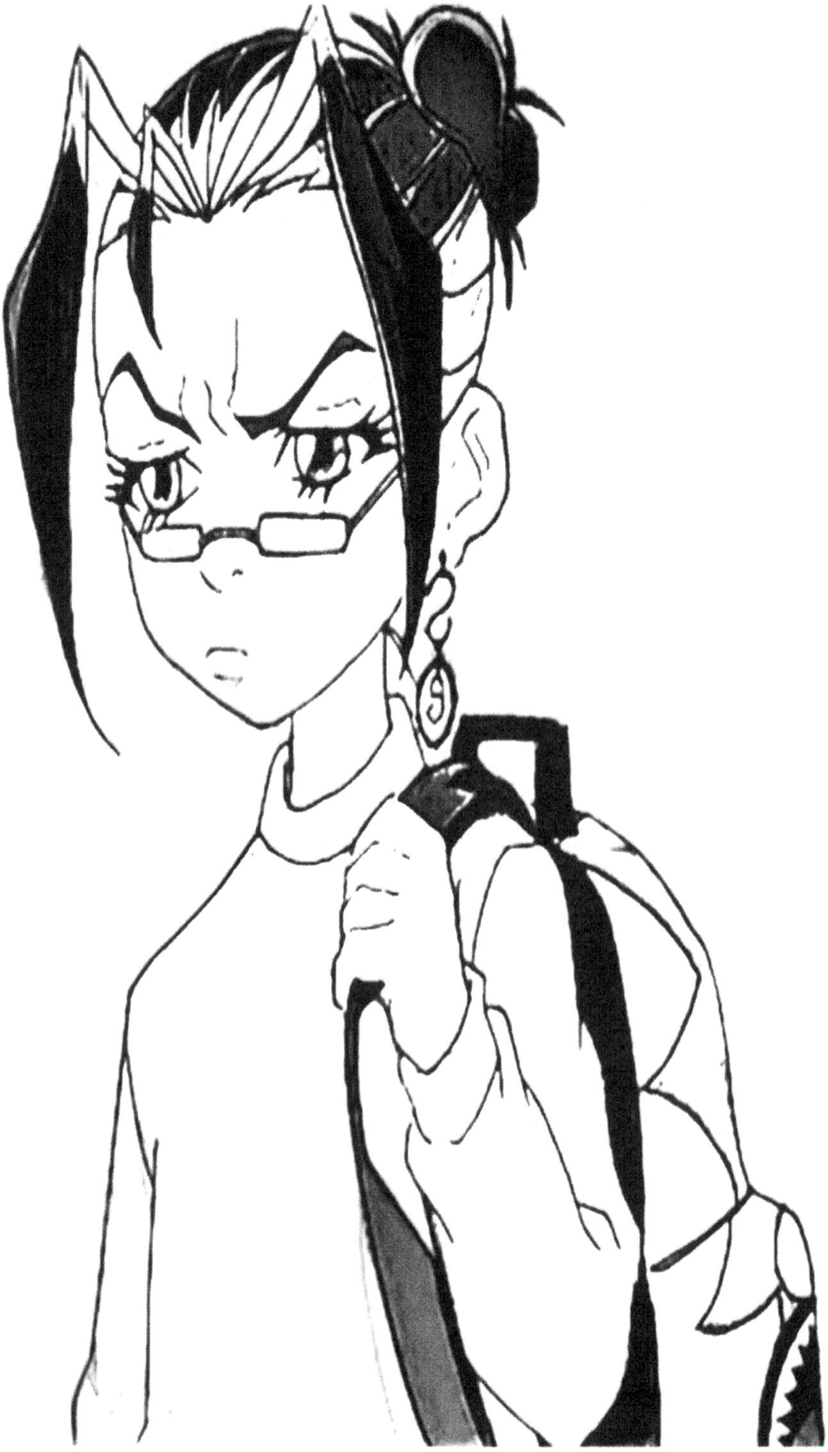

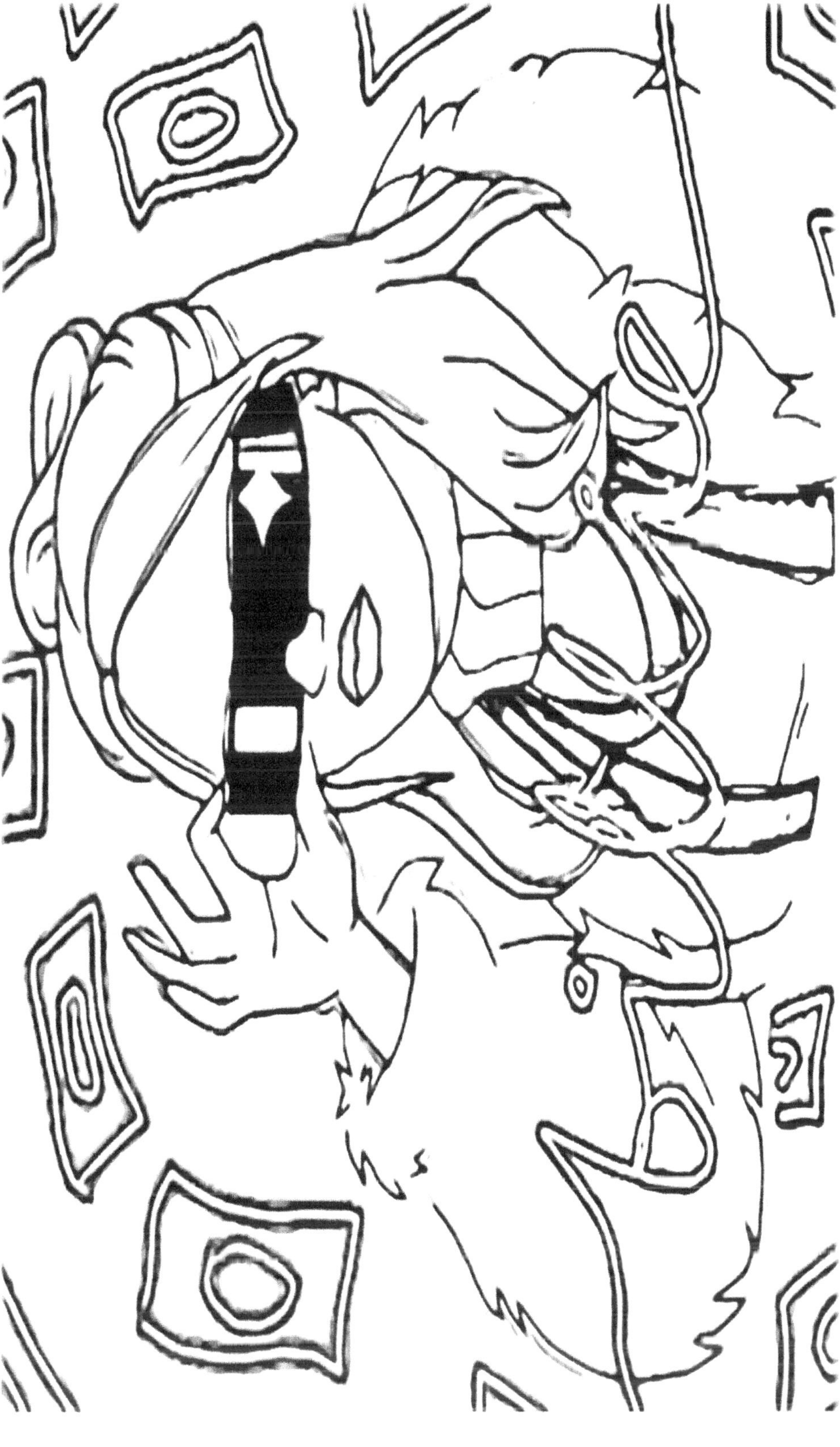

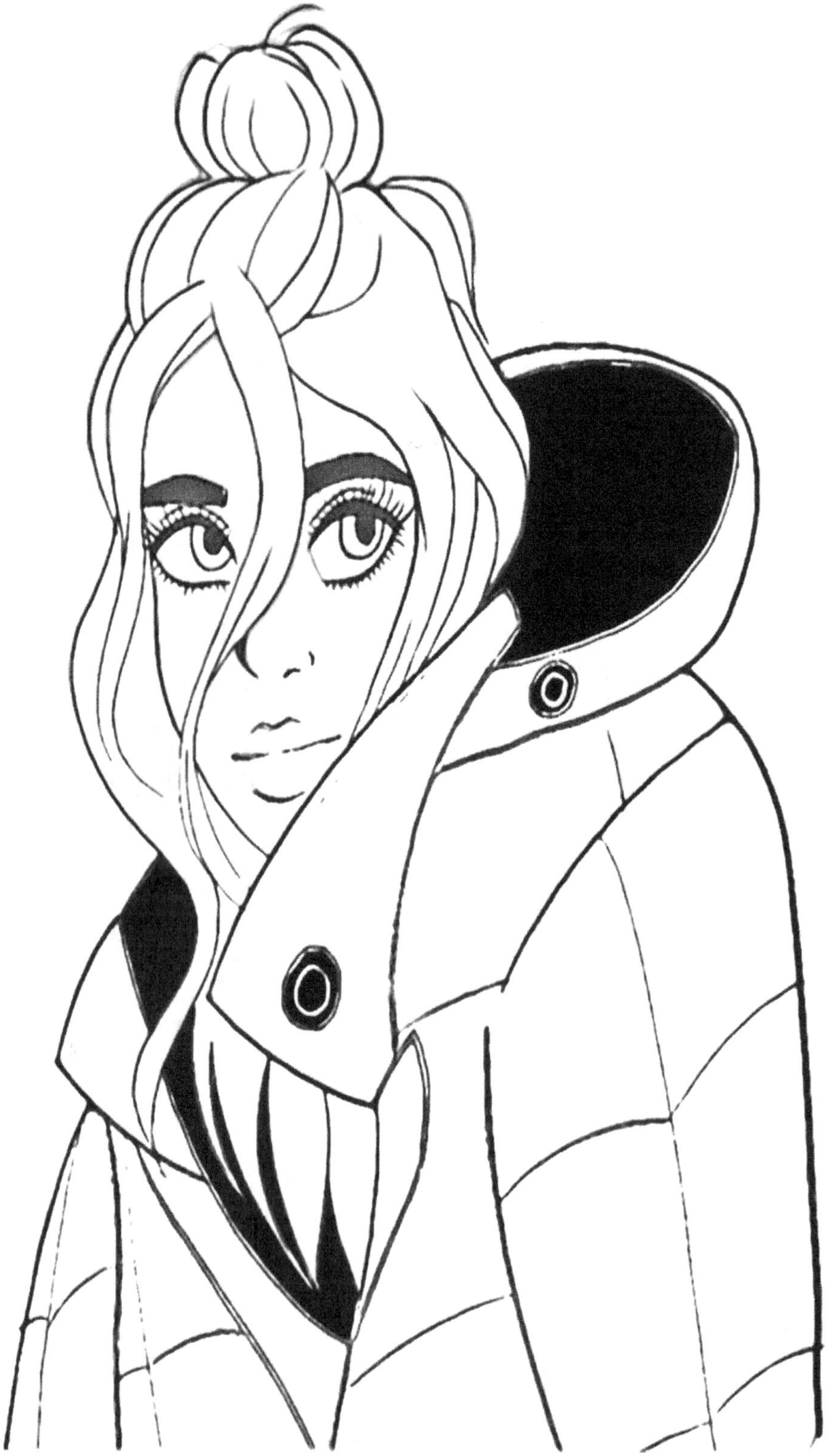

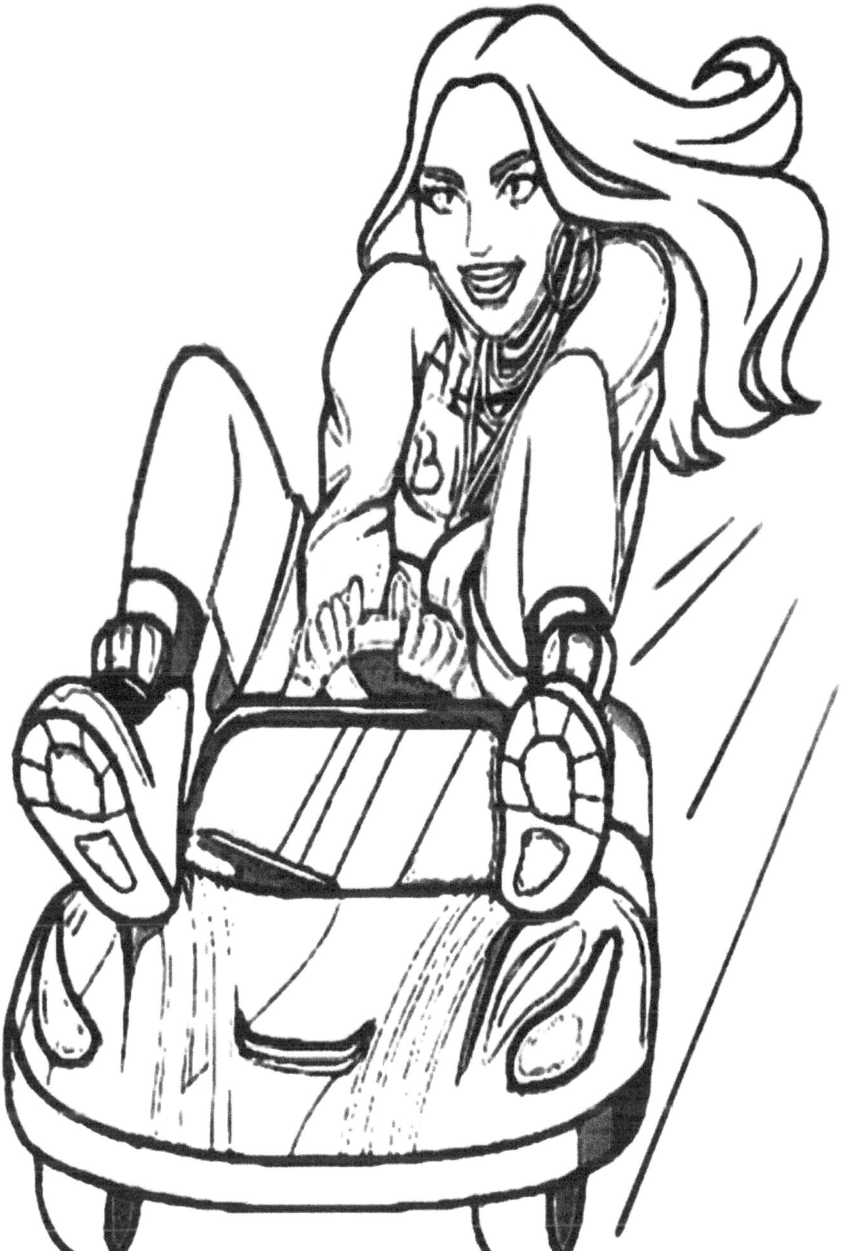

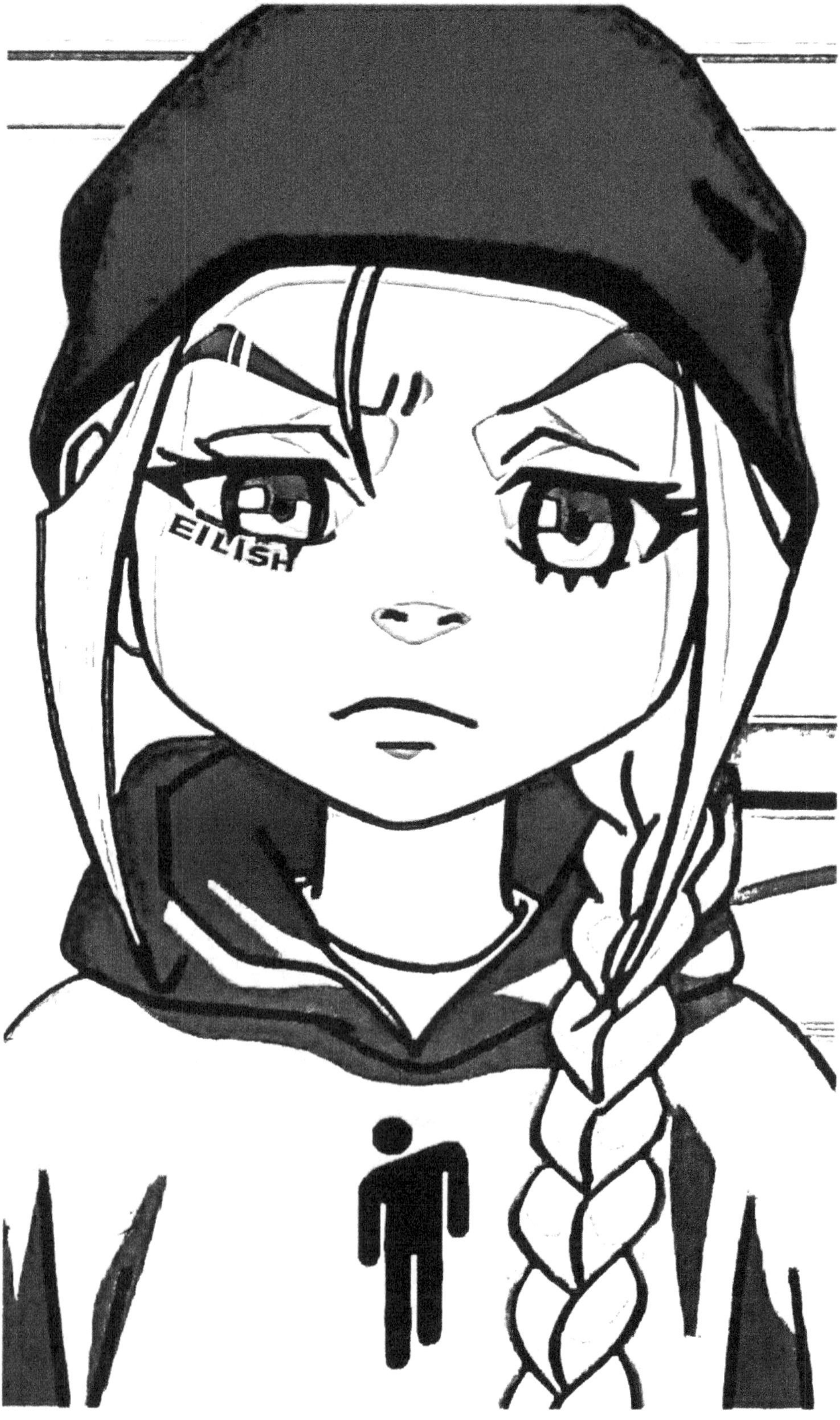
EILISH

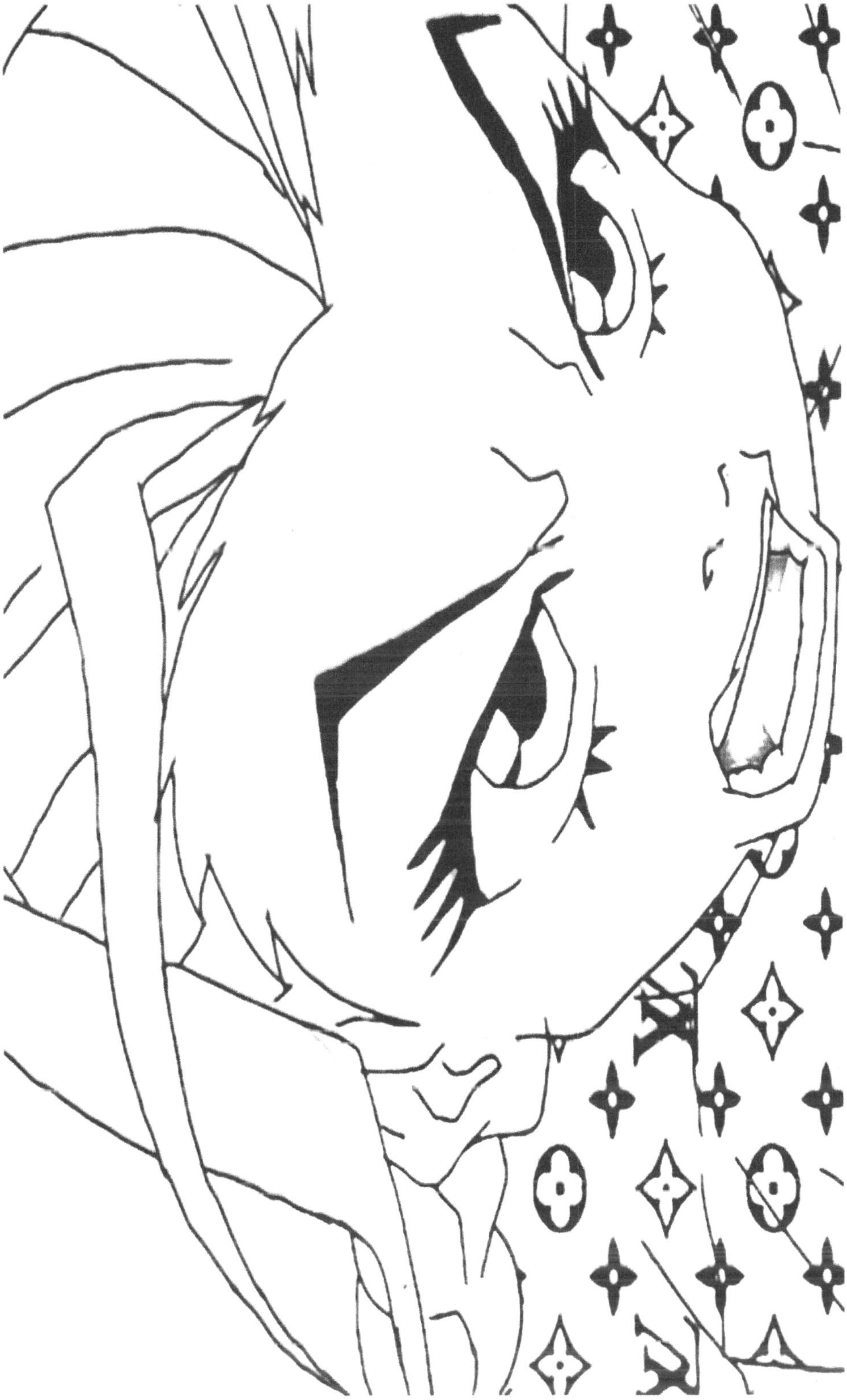

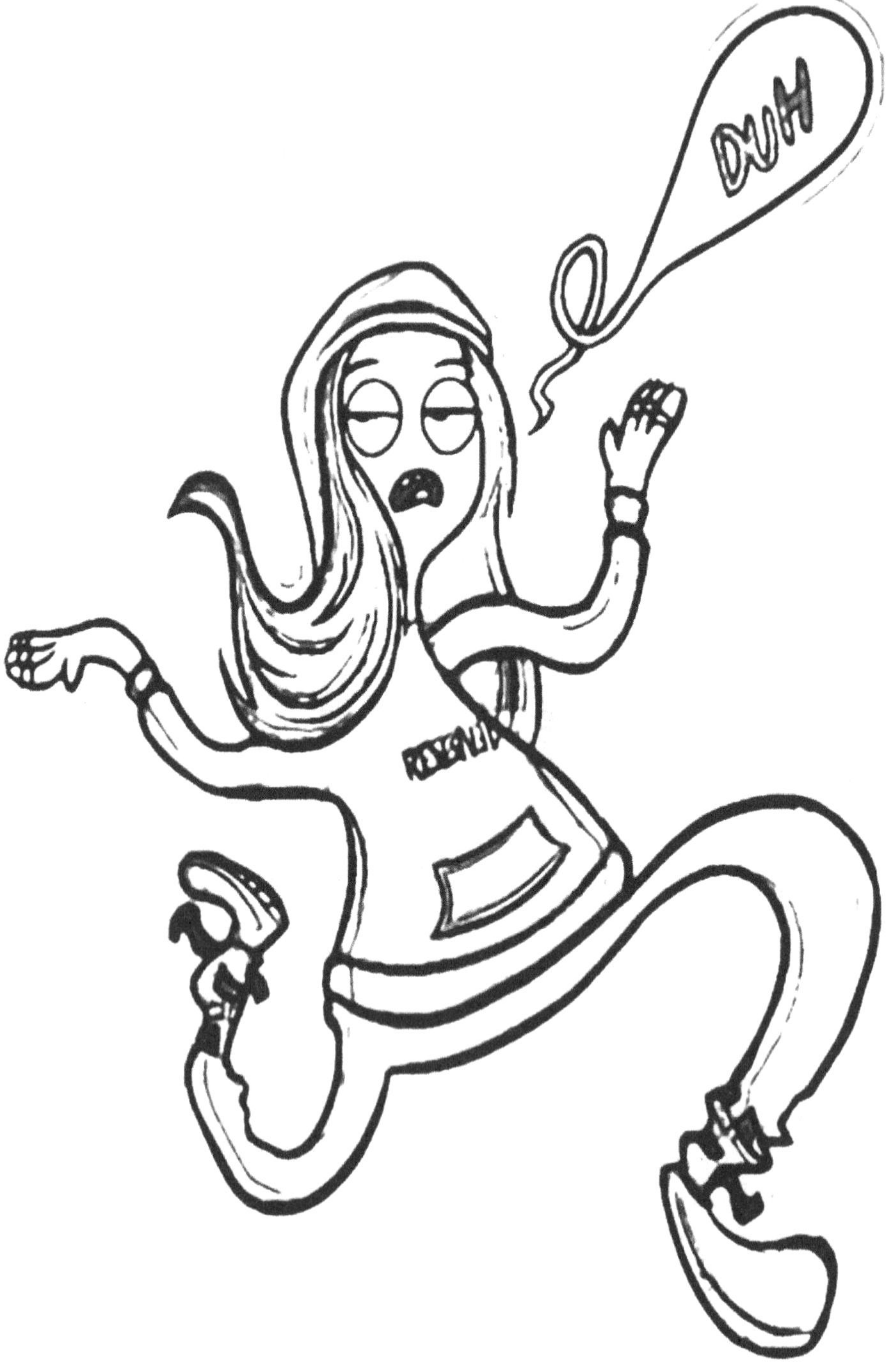
DUH

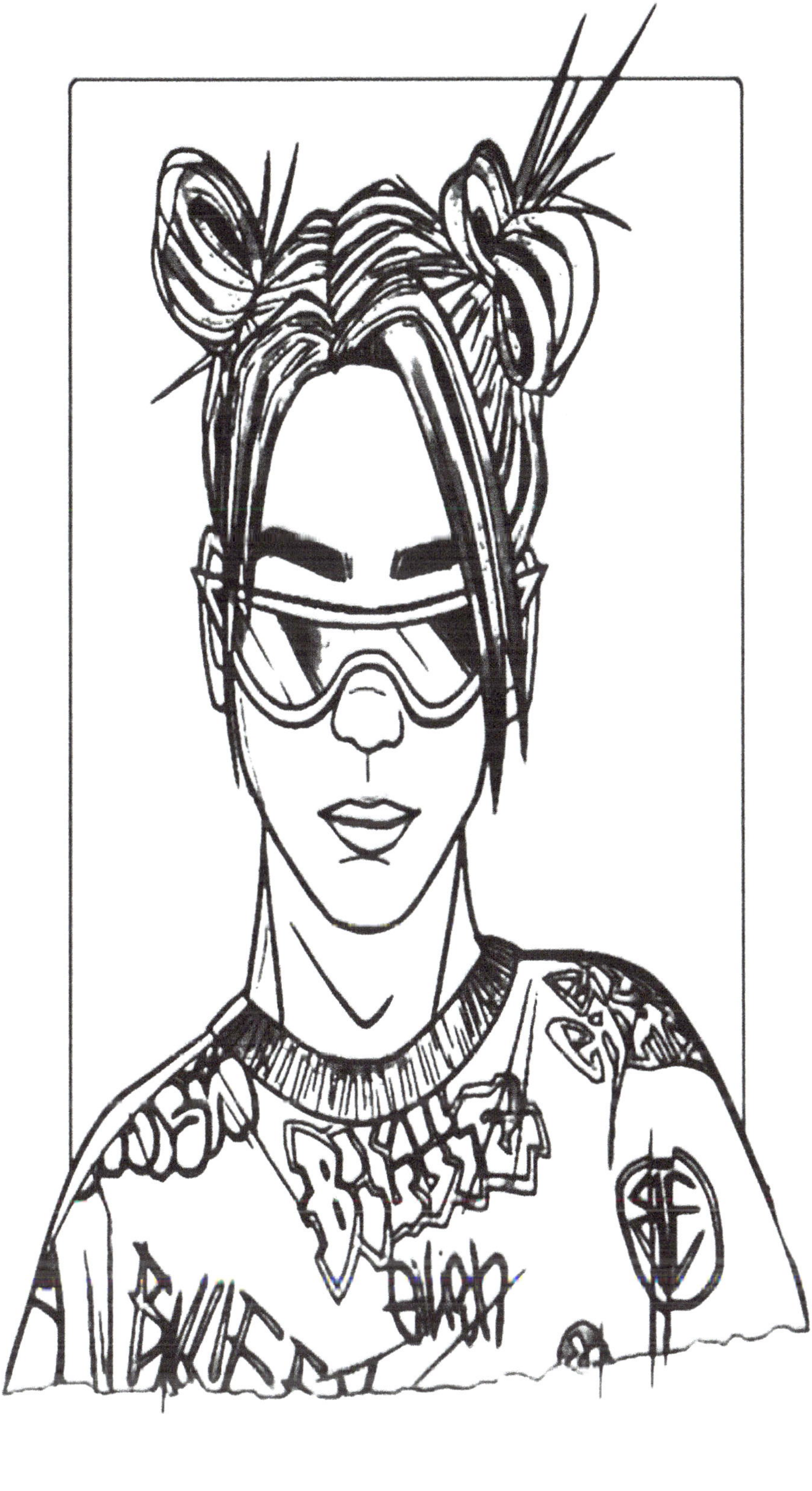

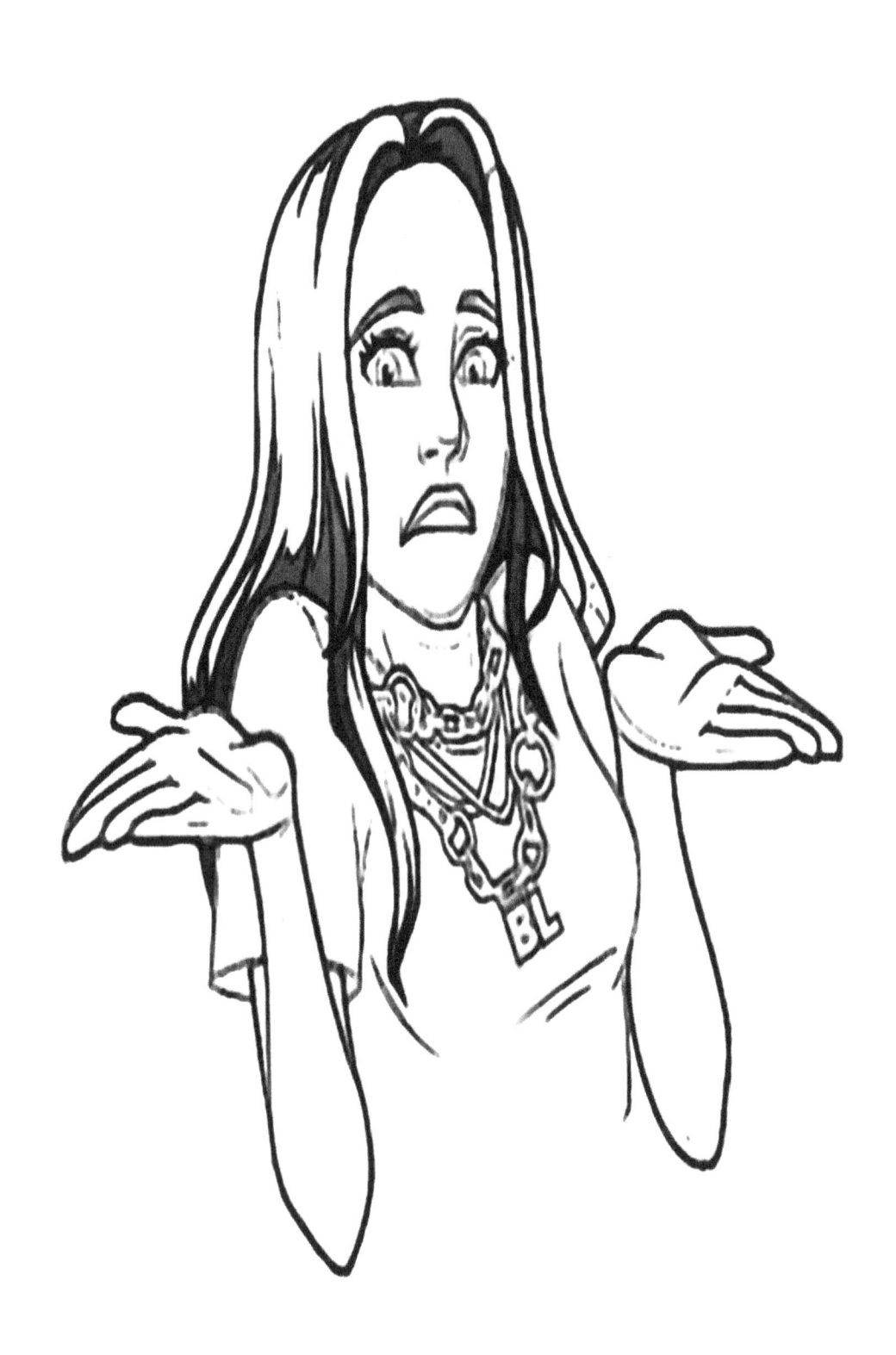
BL

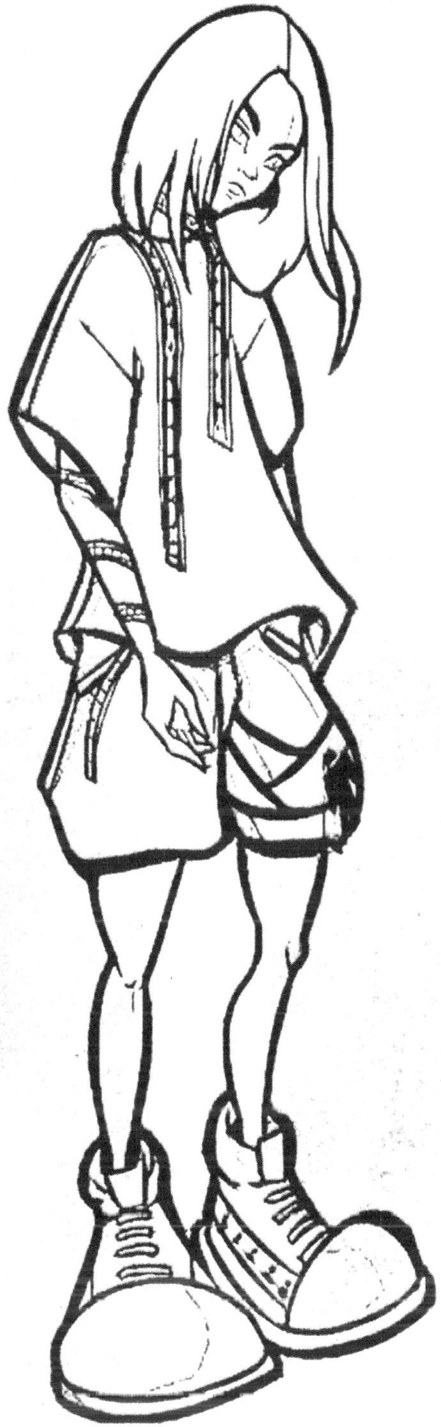

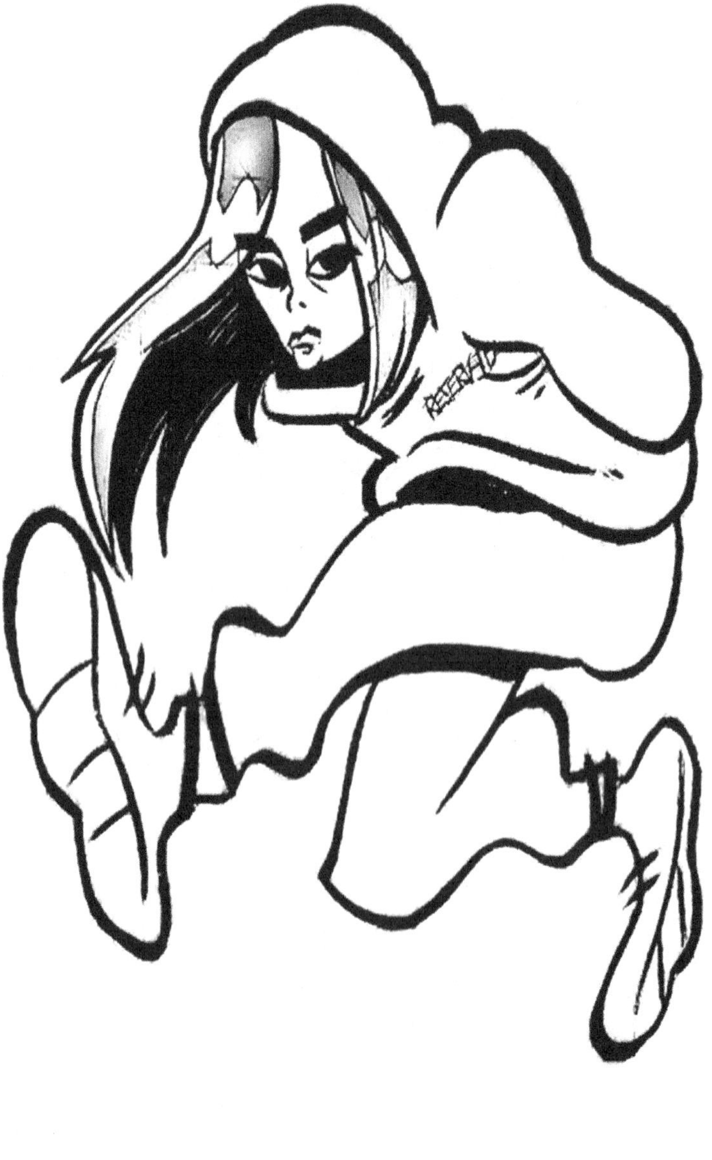

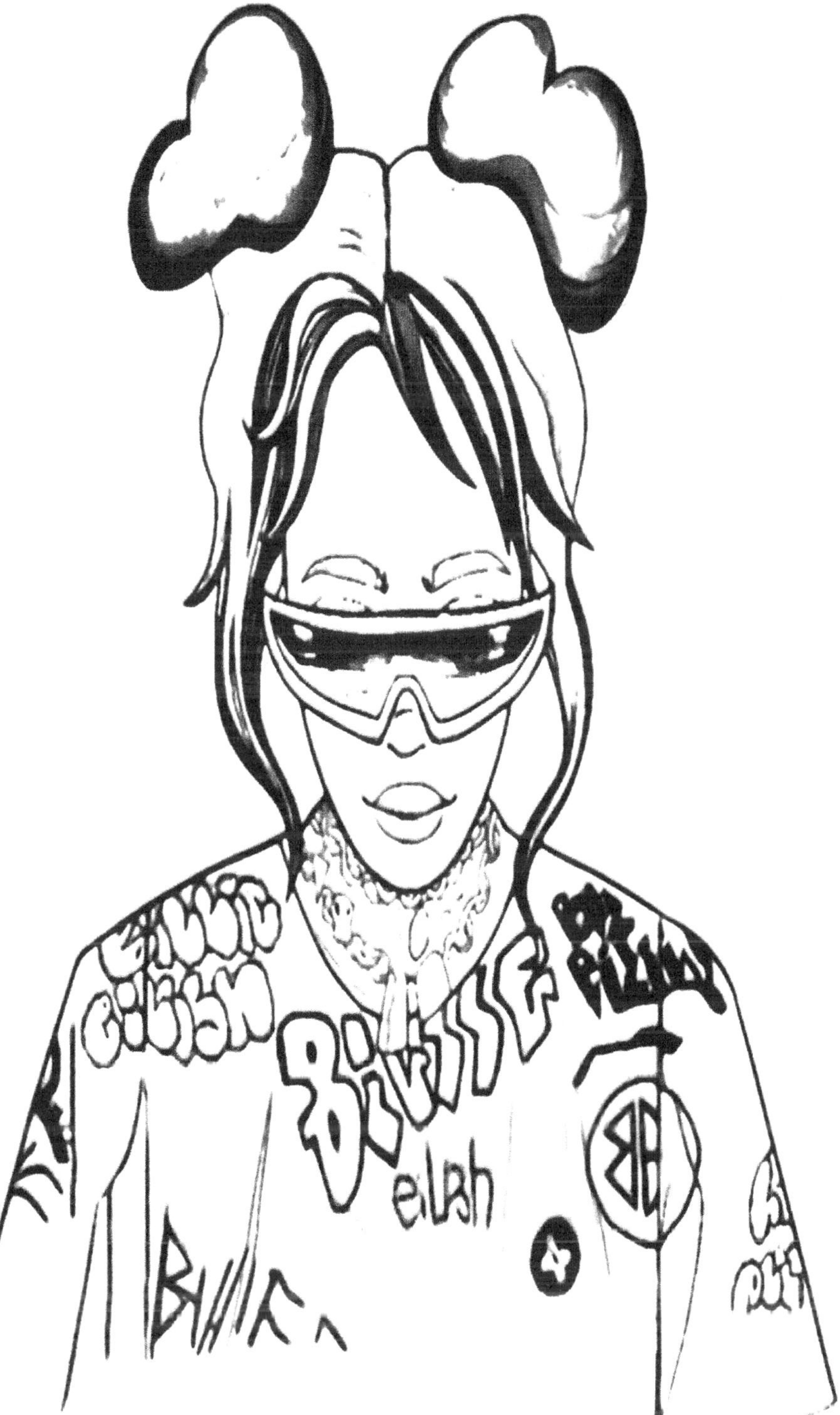

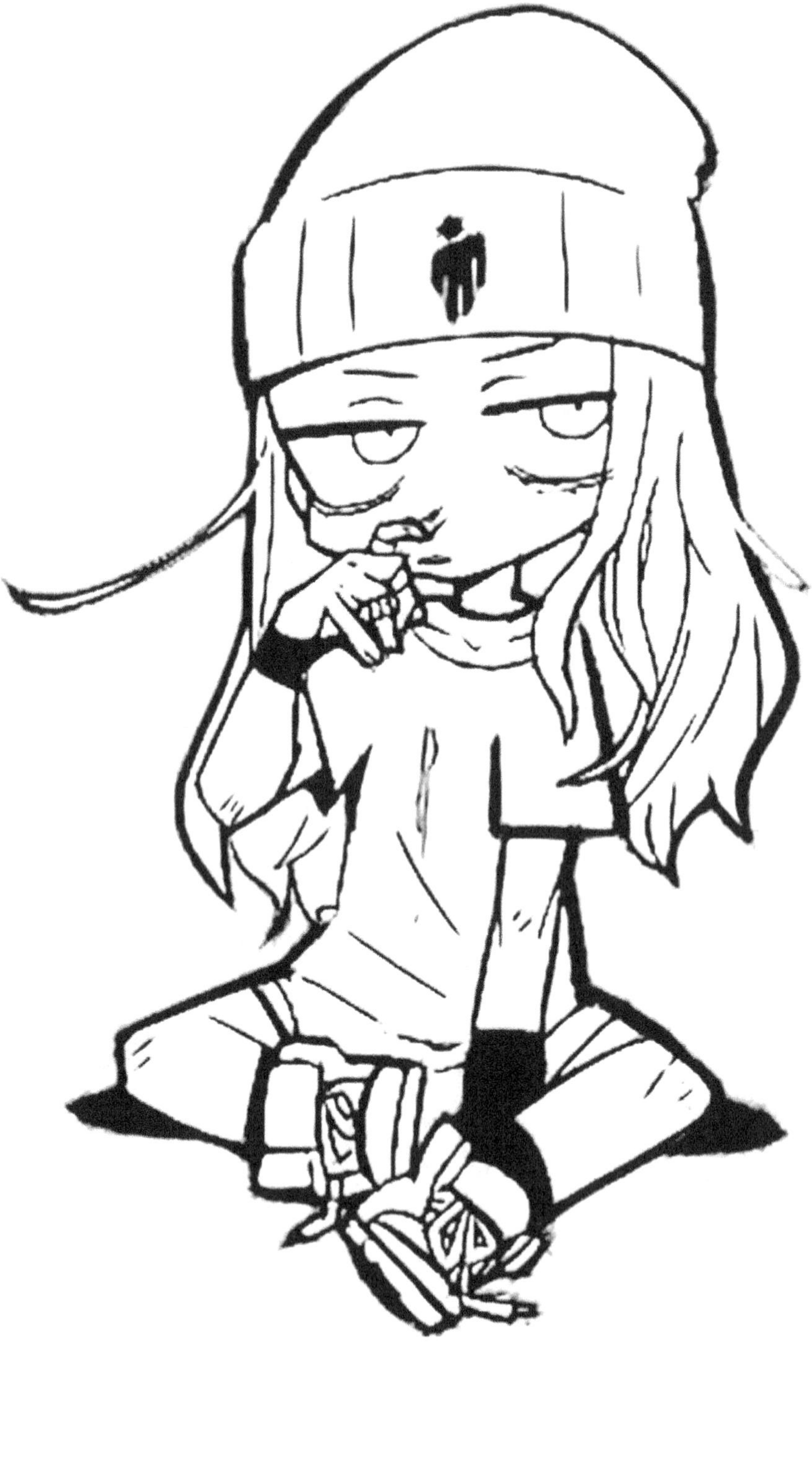

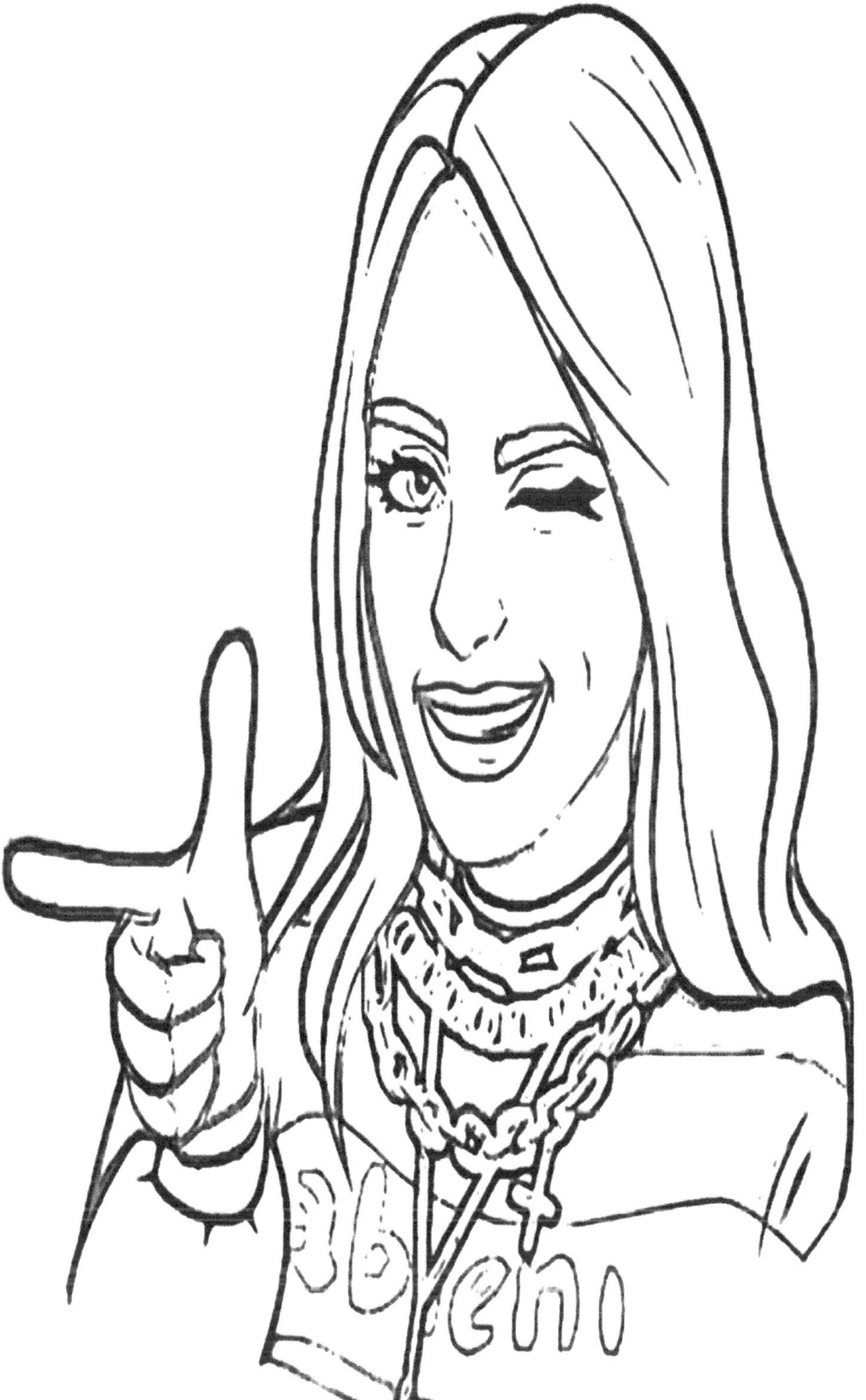

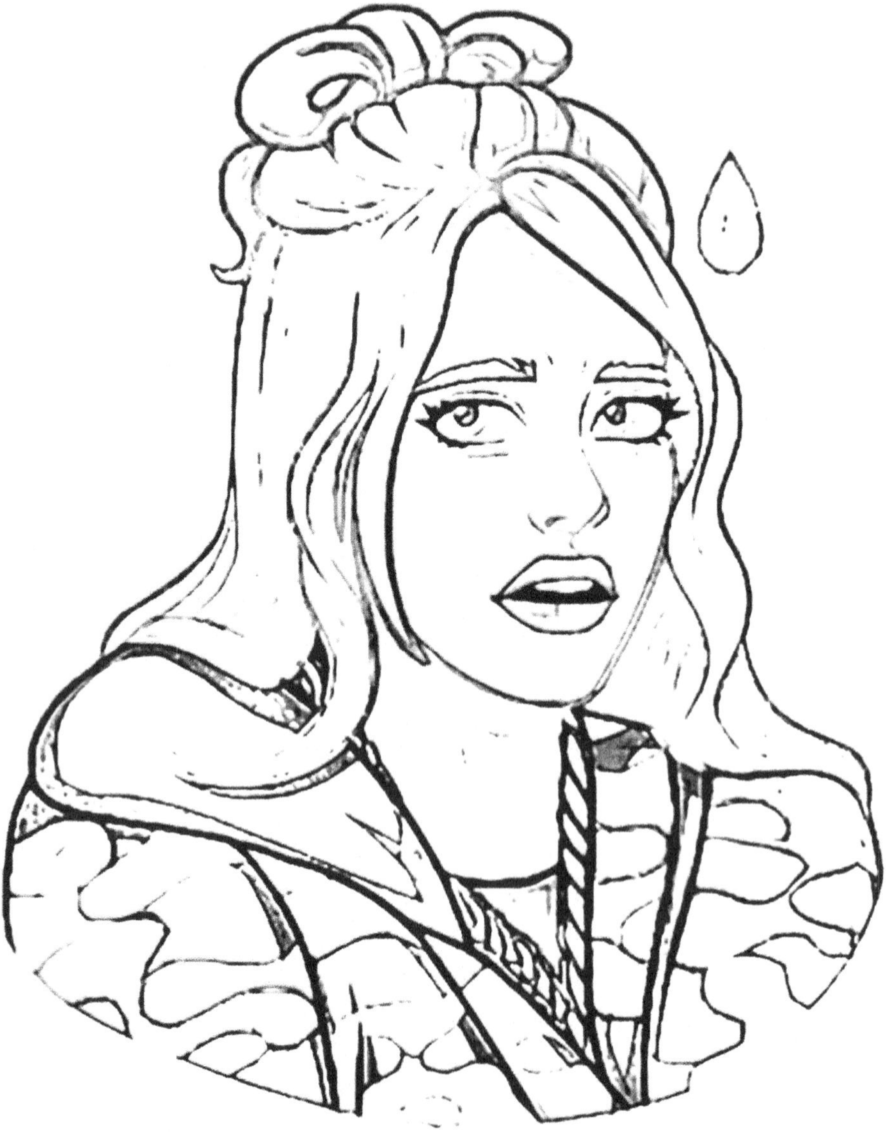

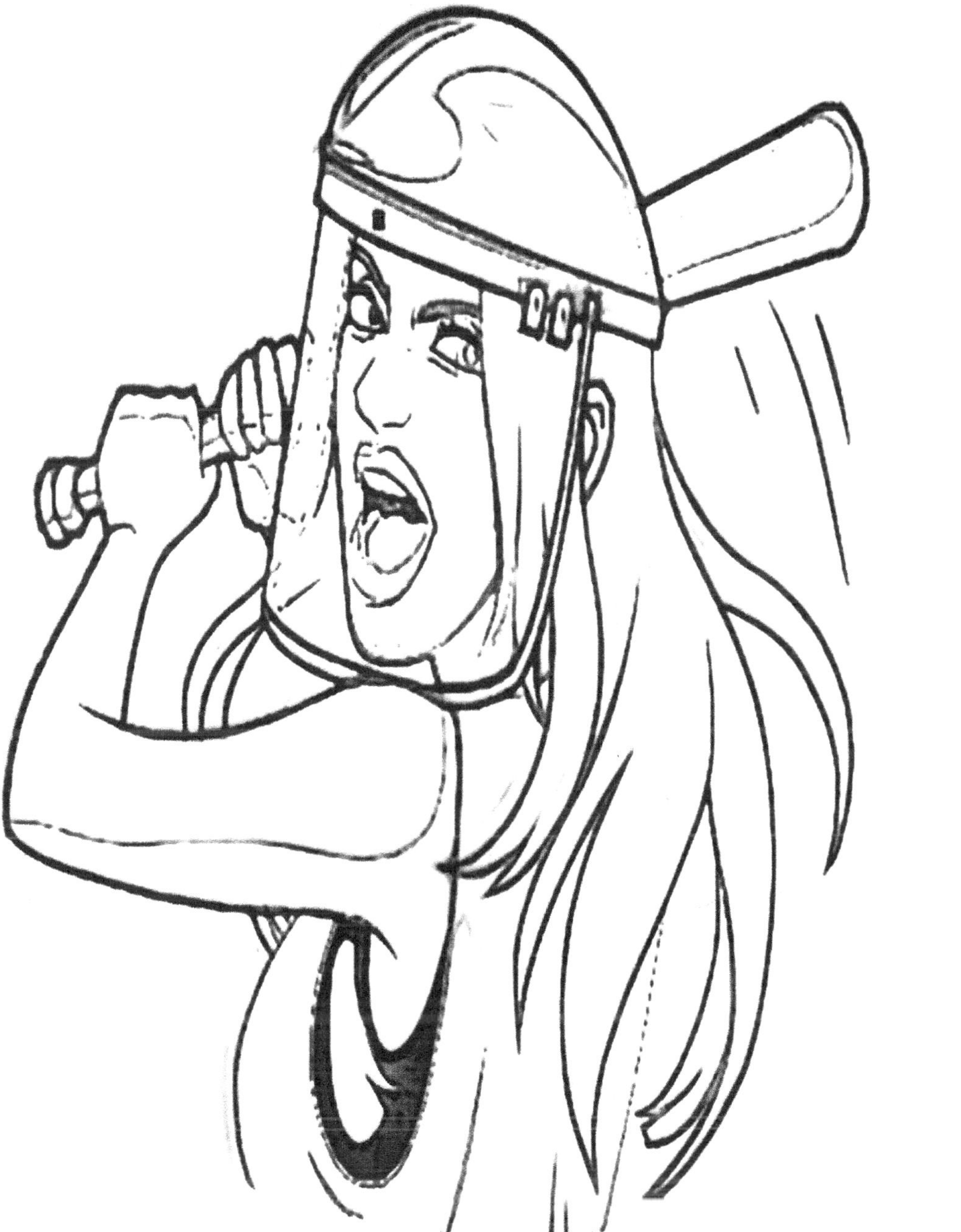

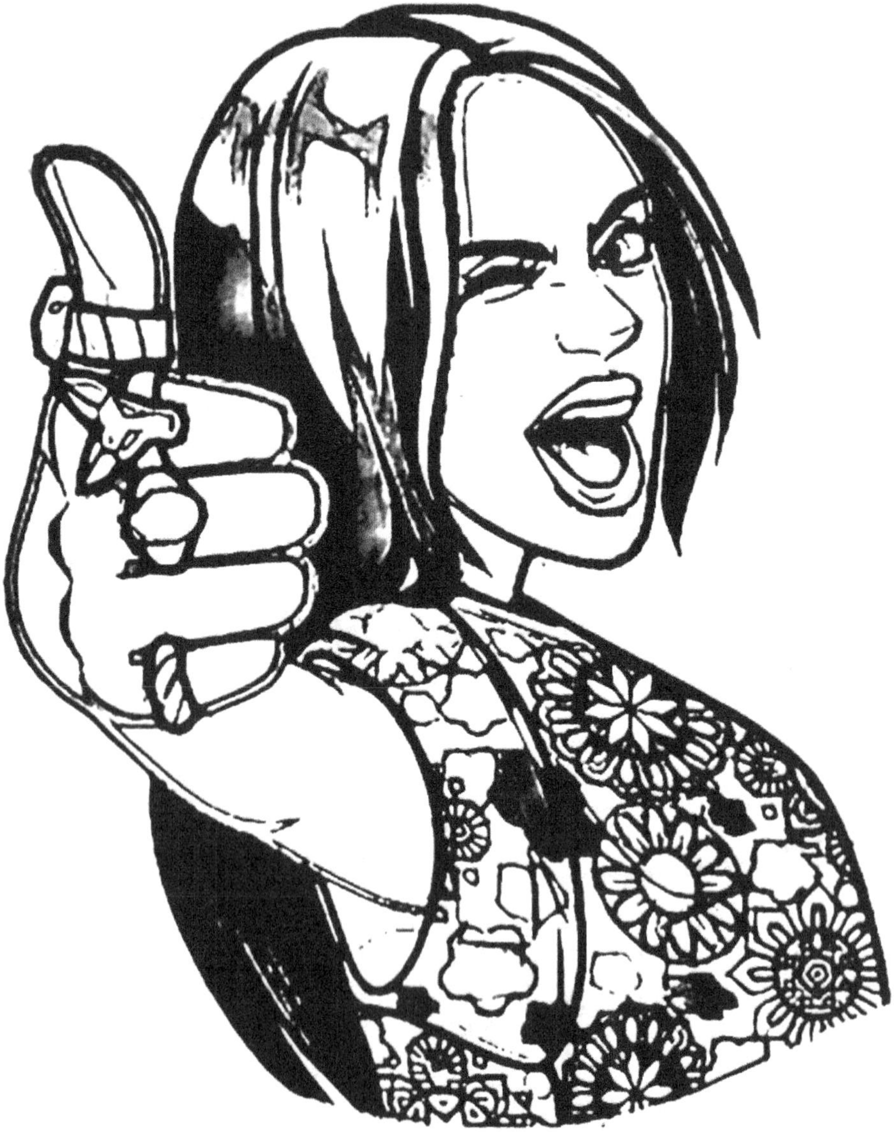

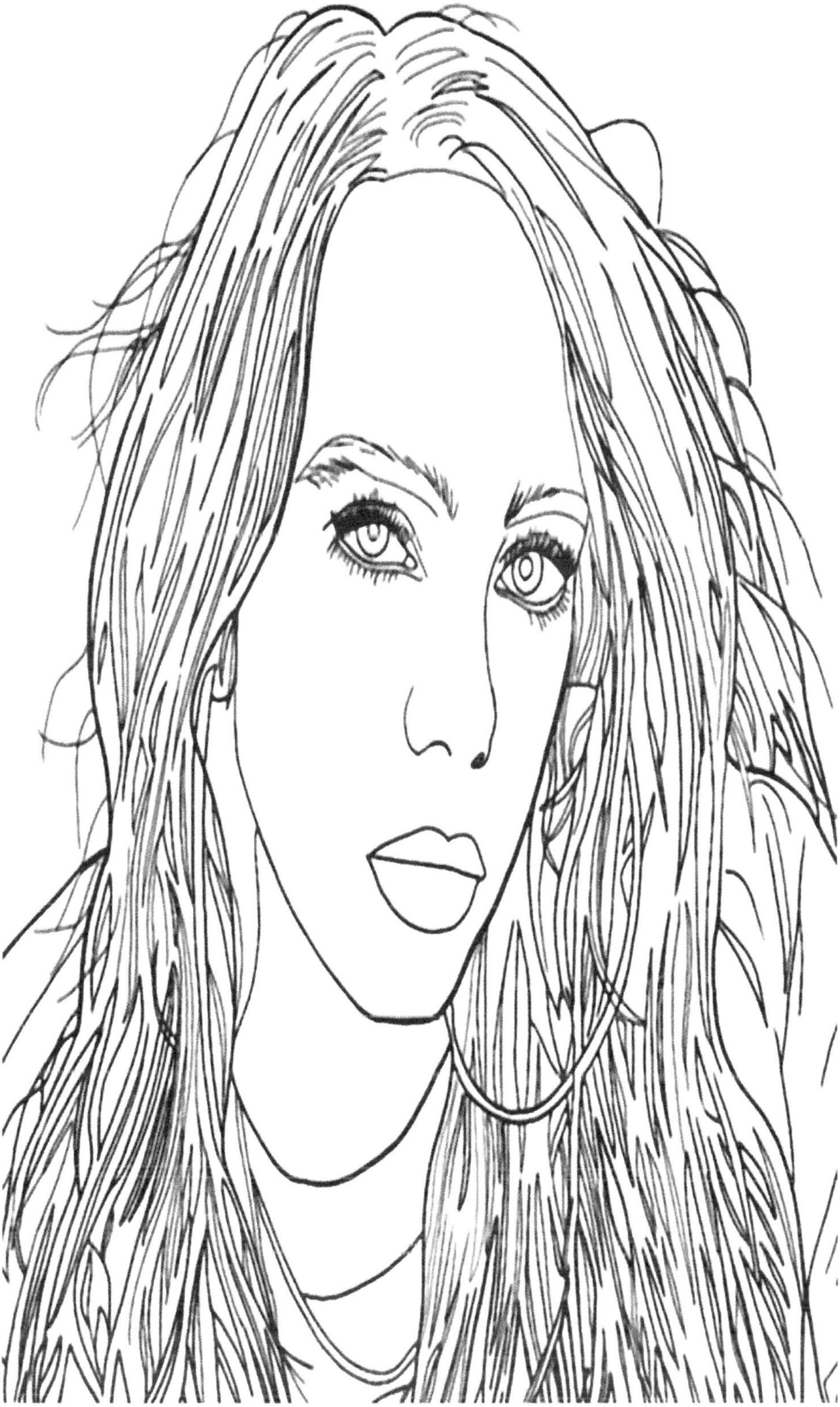

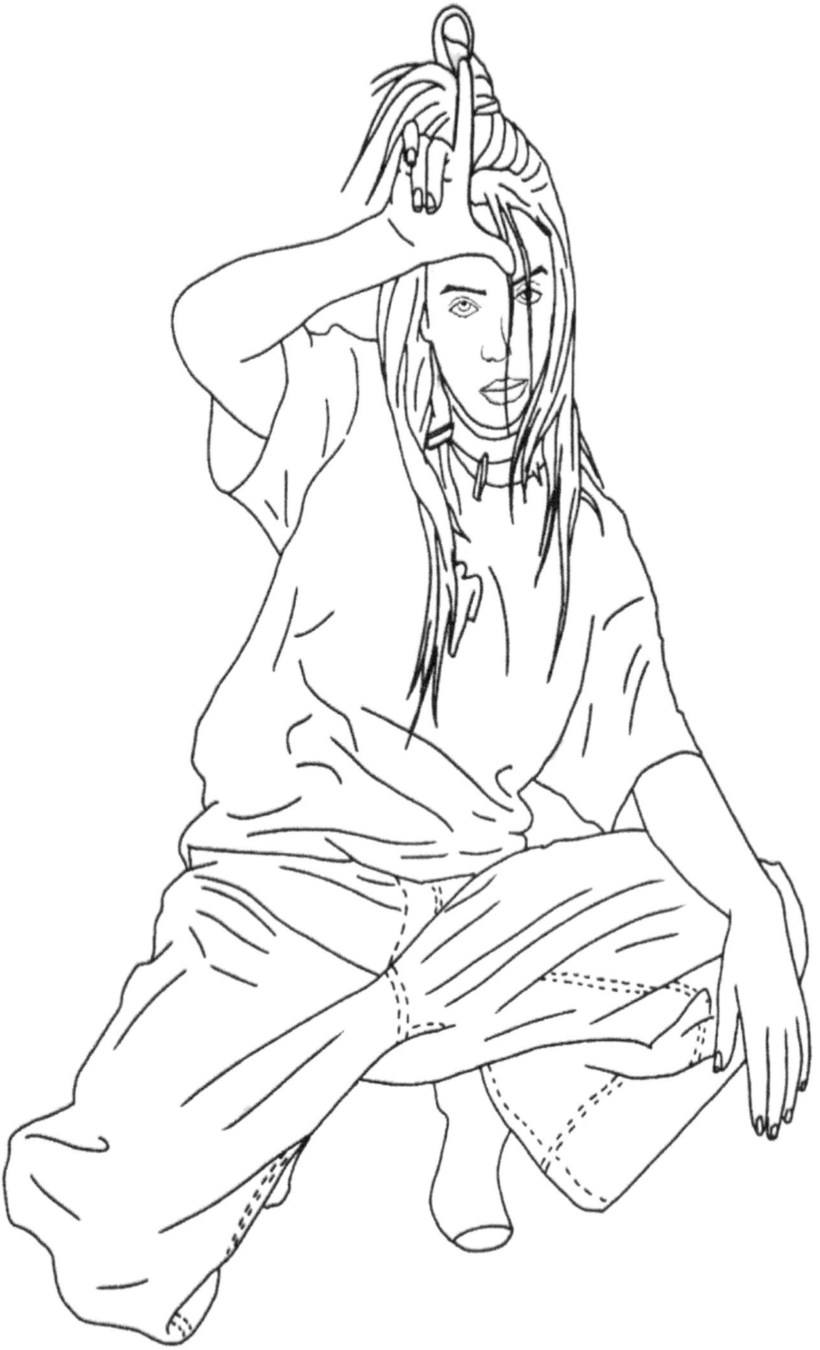

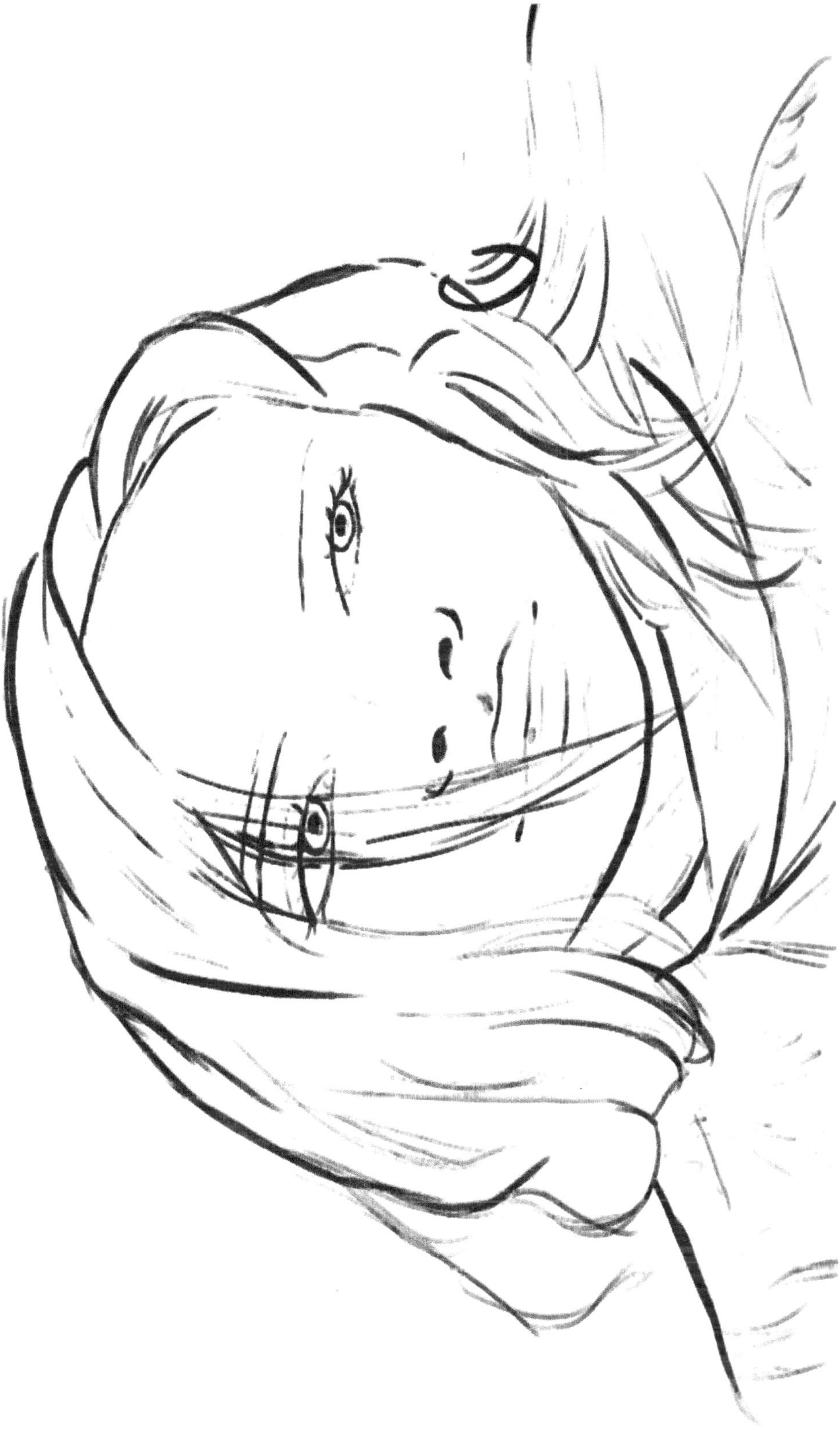

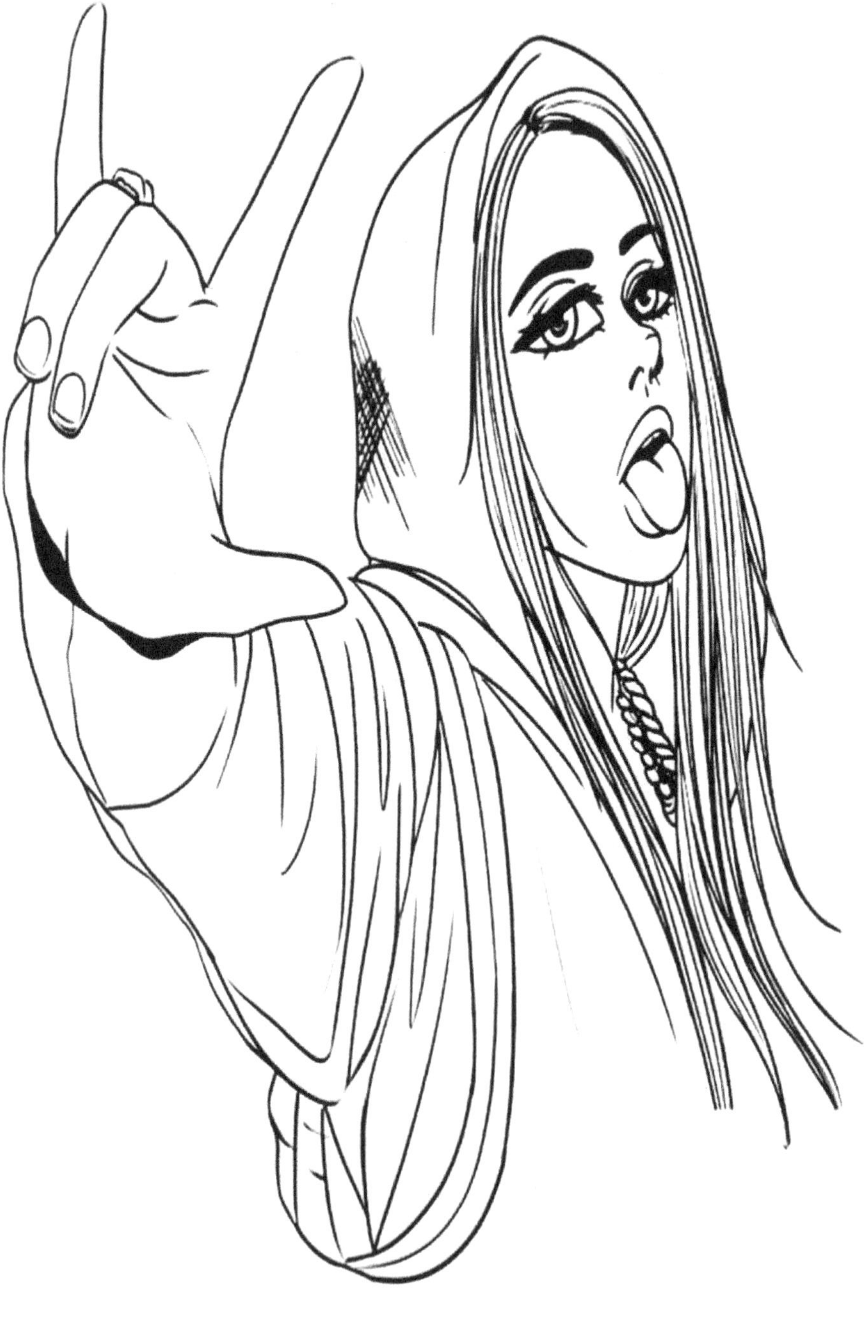

BILLIE EILISH

WHEN WE ALL FALL ASLEEP, WHERE DO WE GO?

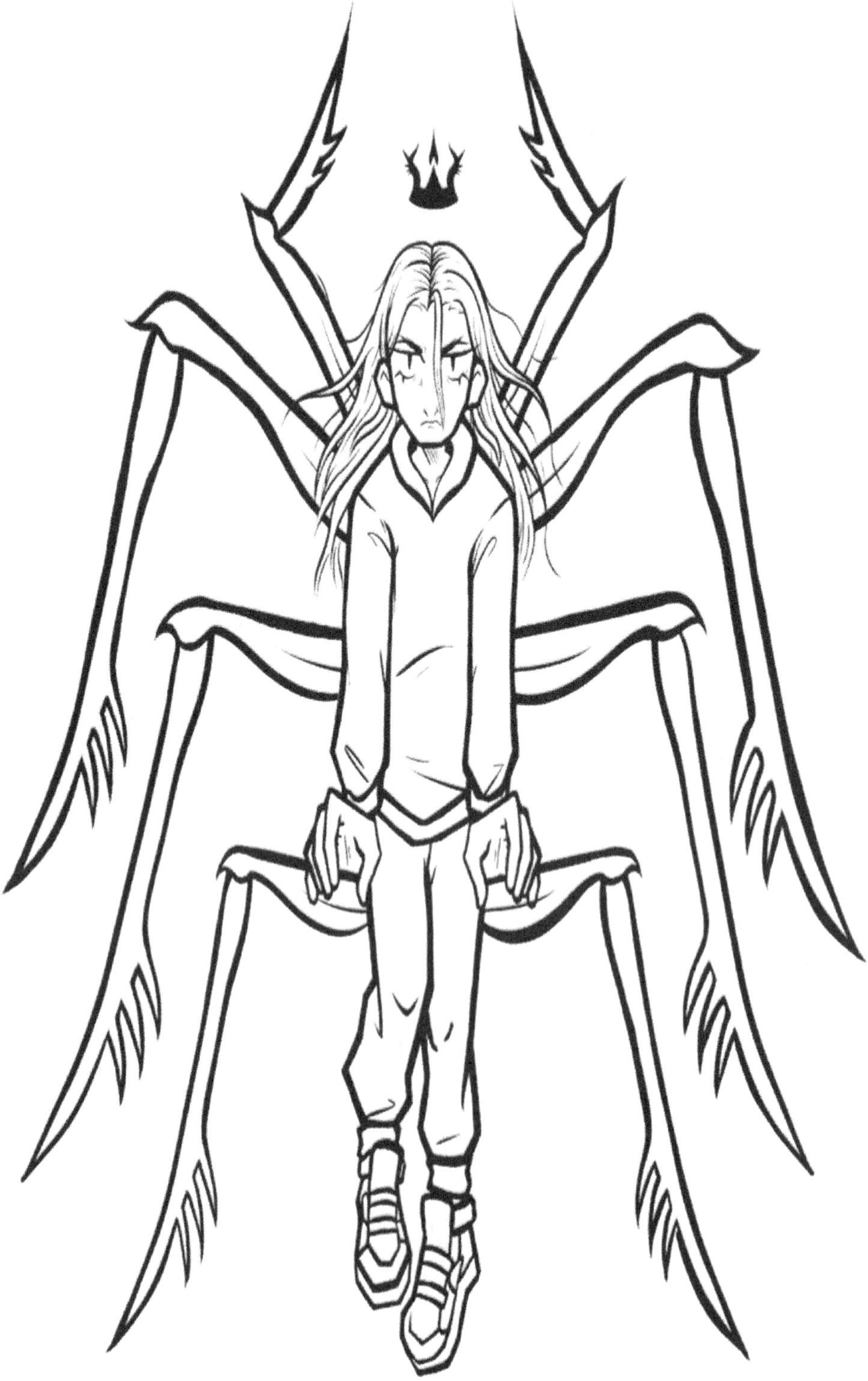

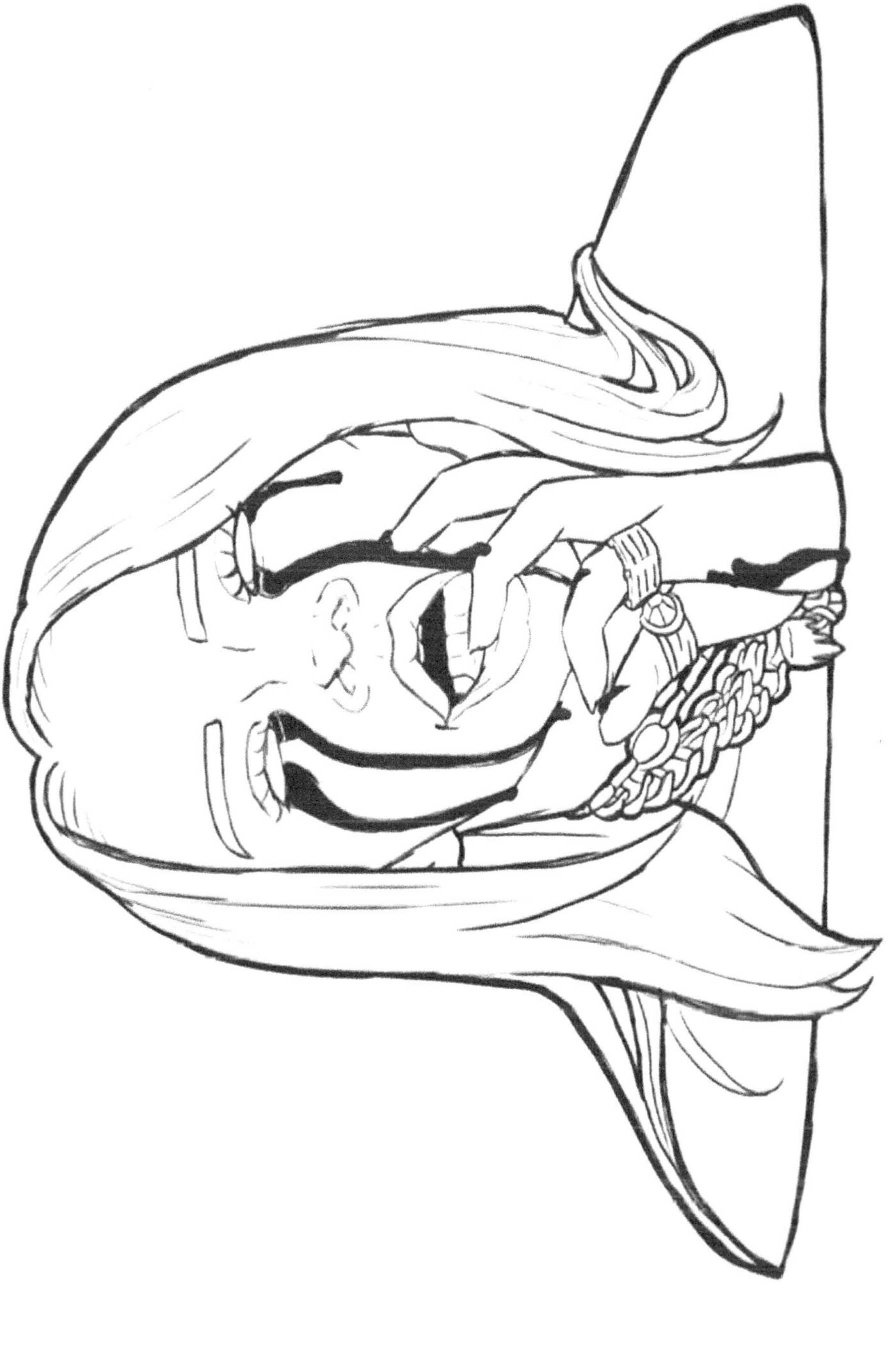

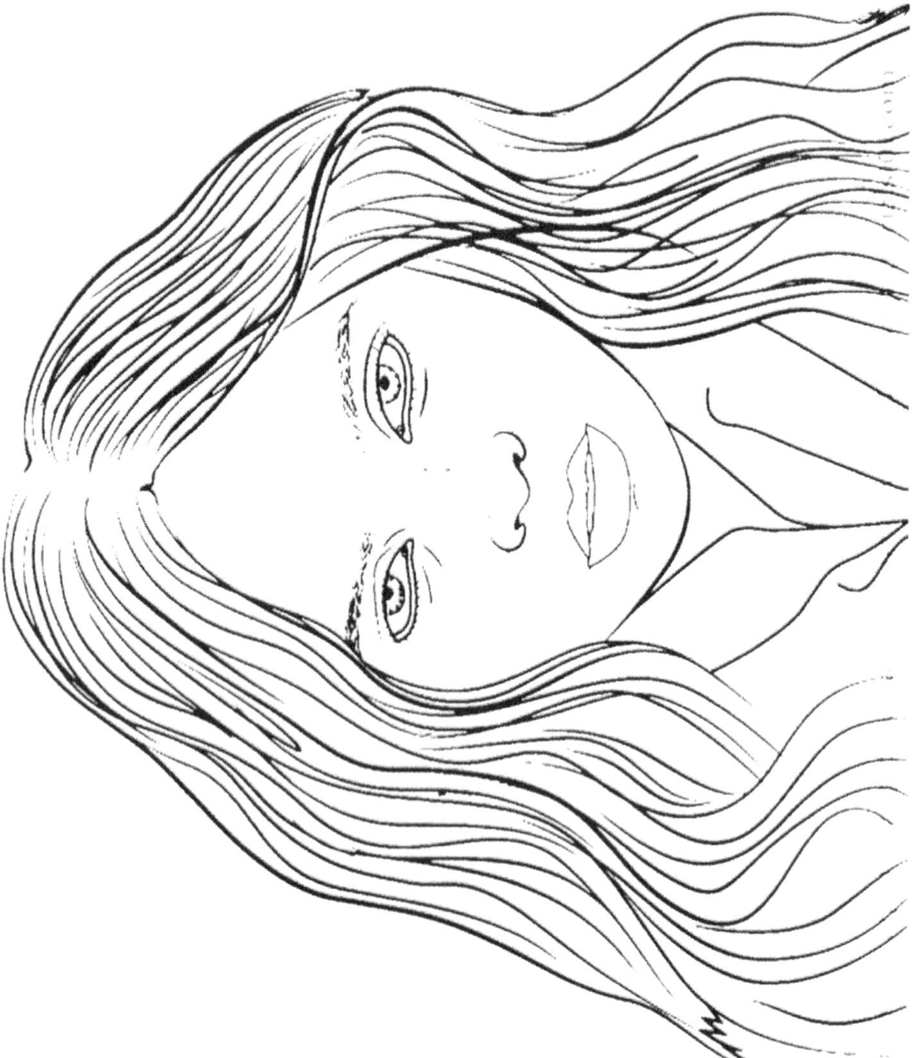

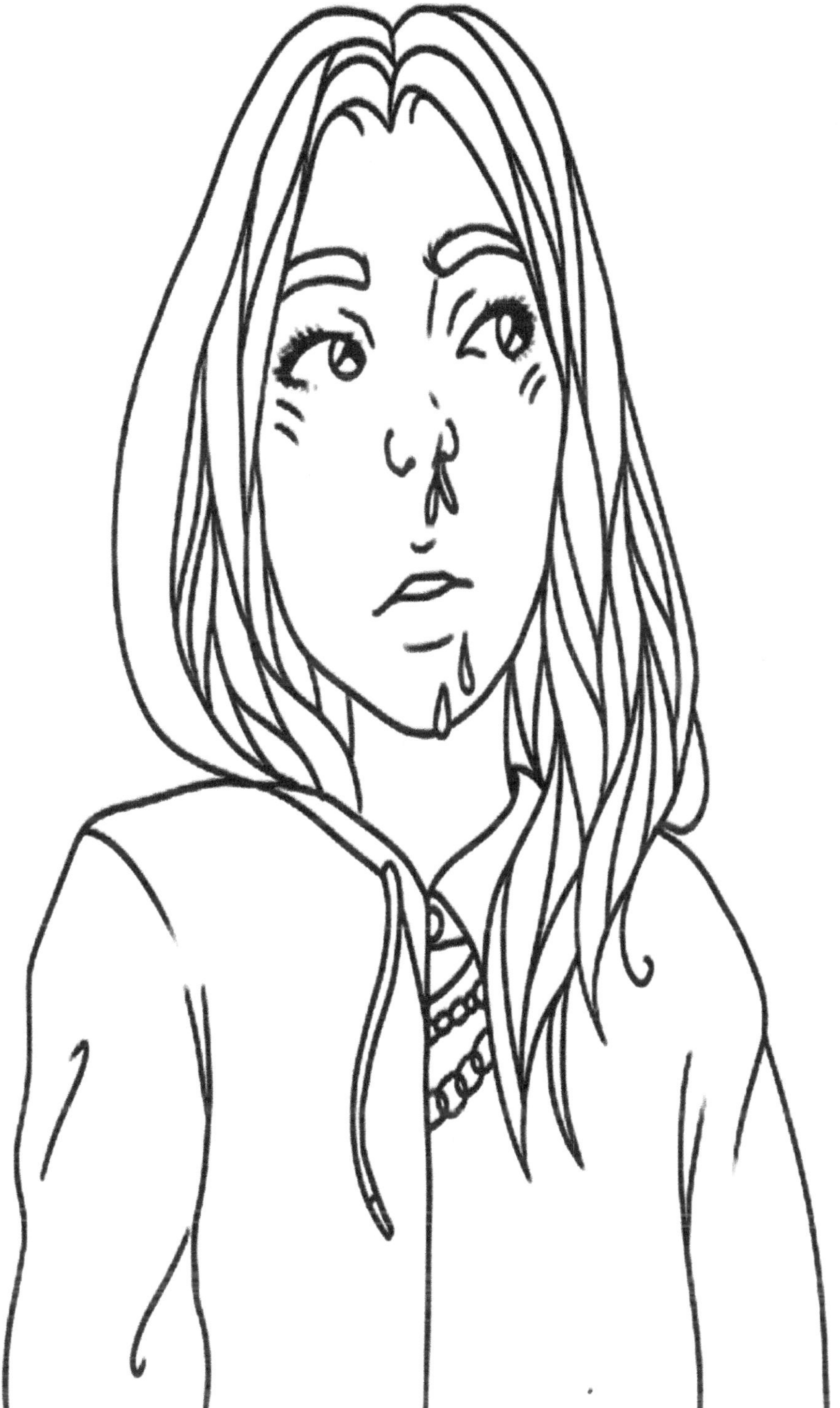

call me friend
but keep me closer

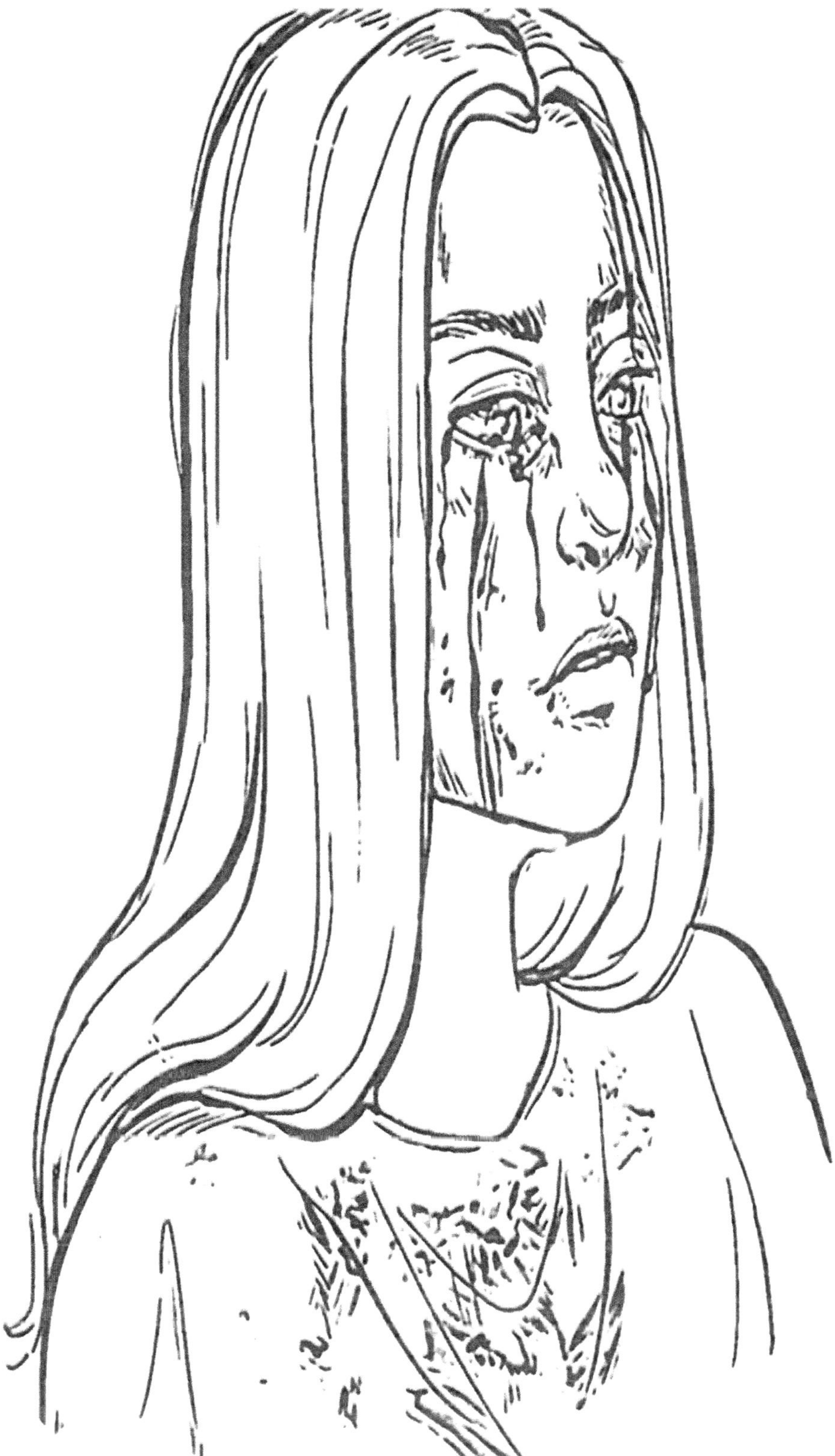

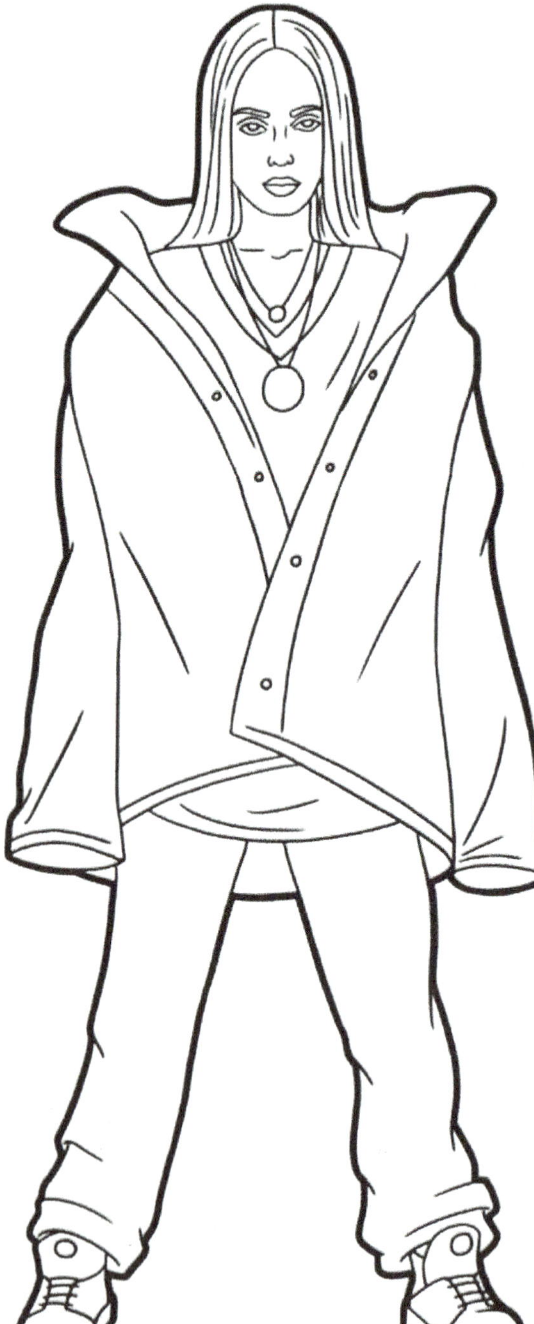

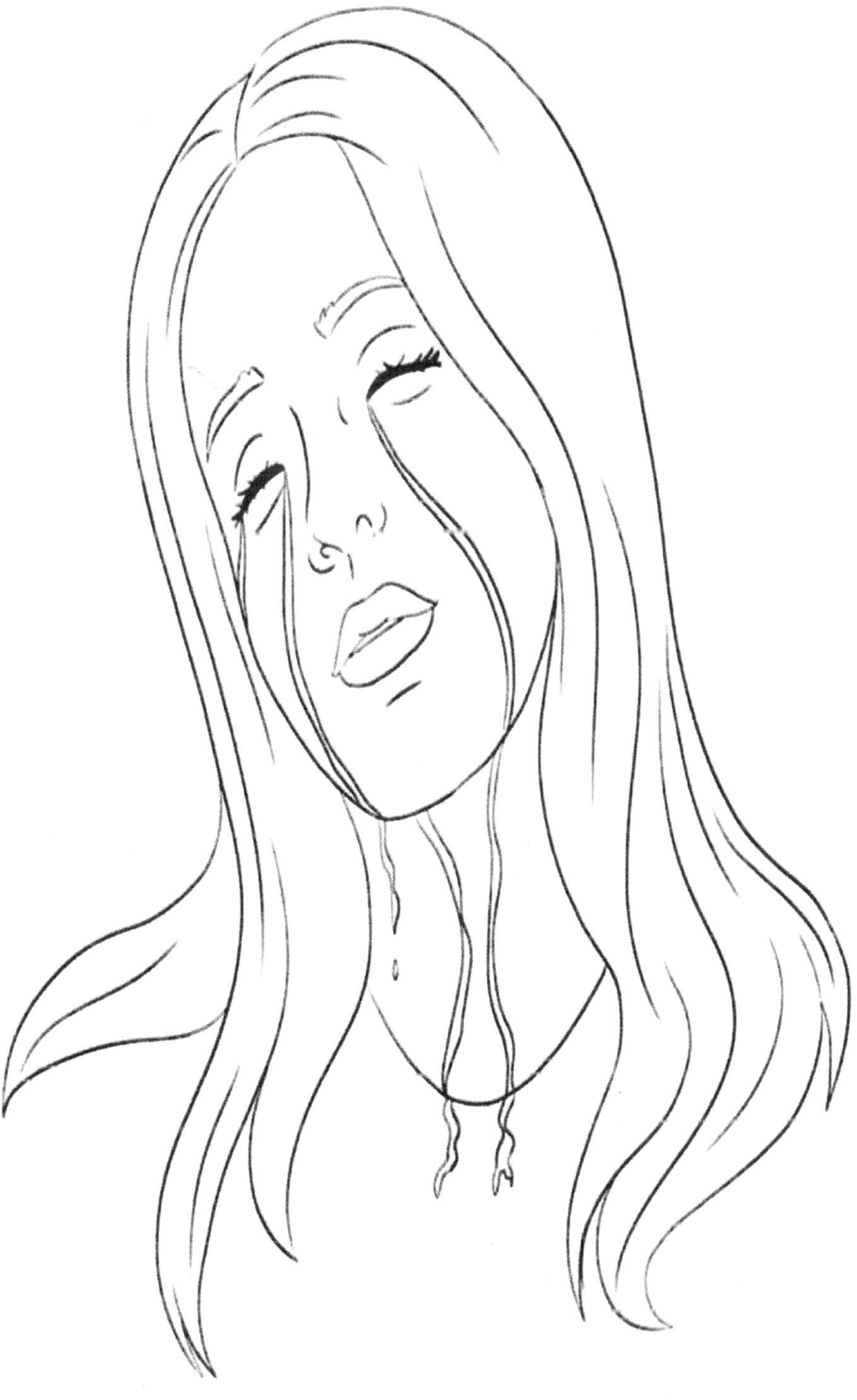

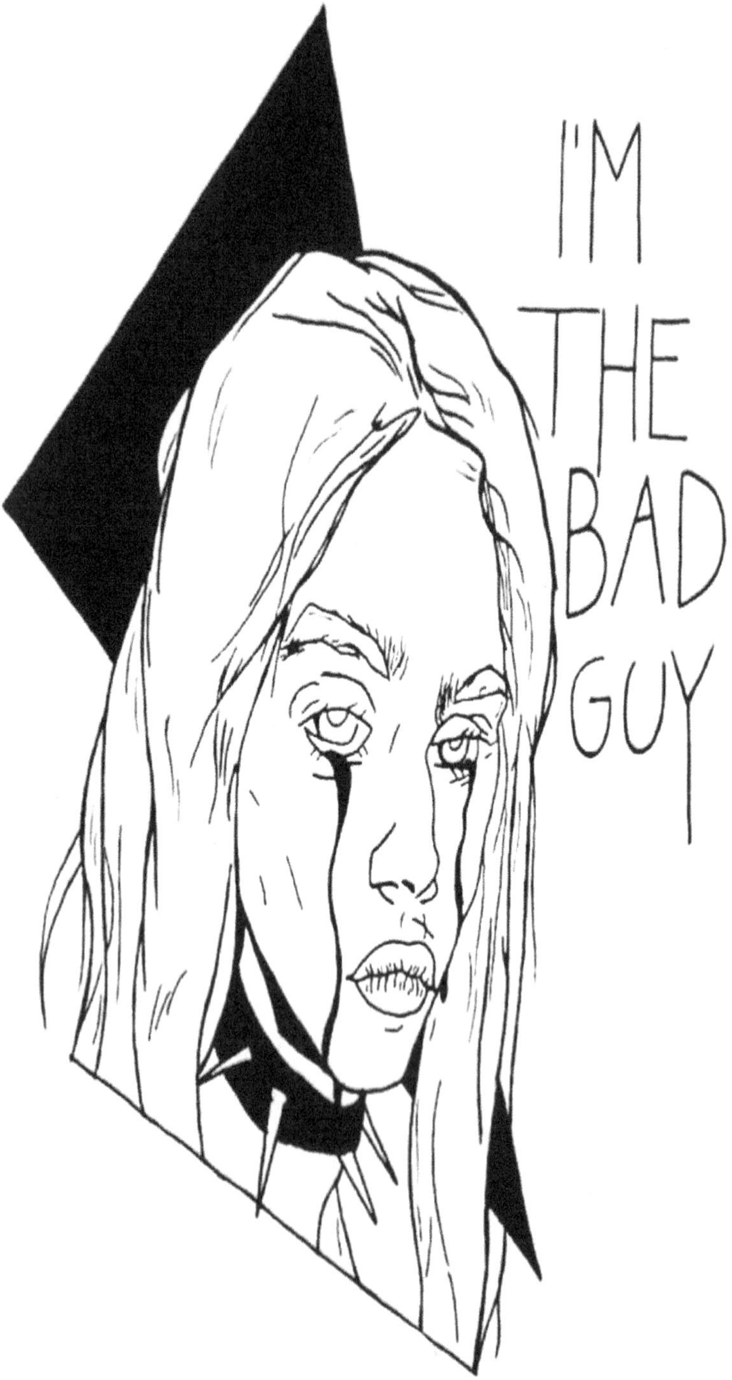
I'M THE BAD GUY

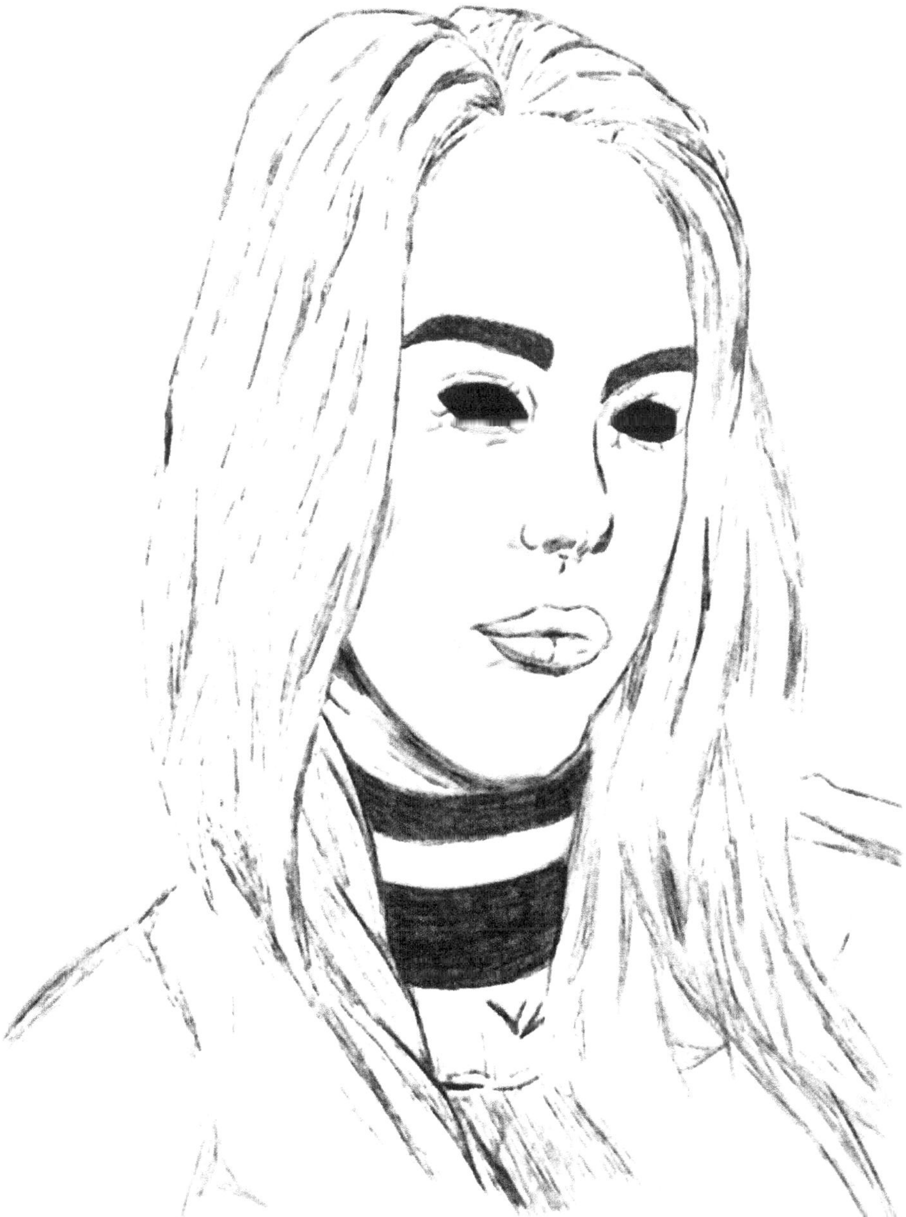

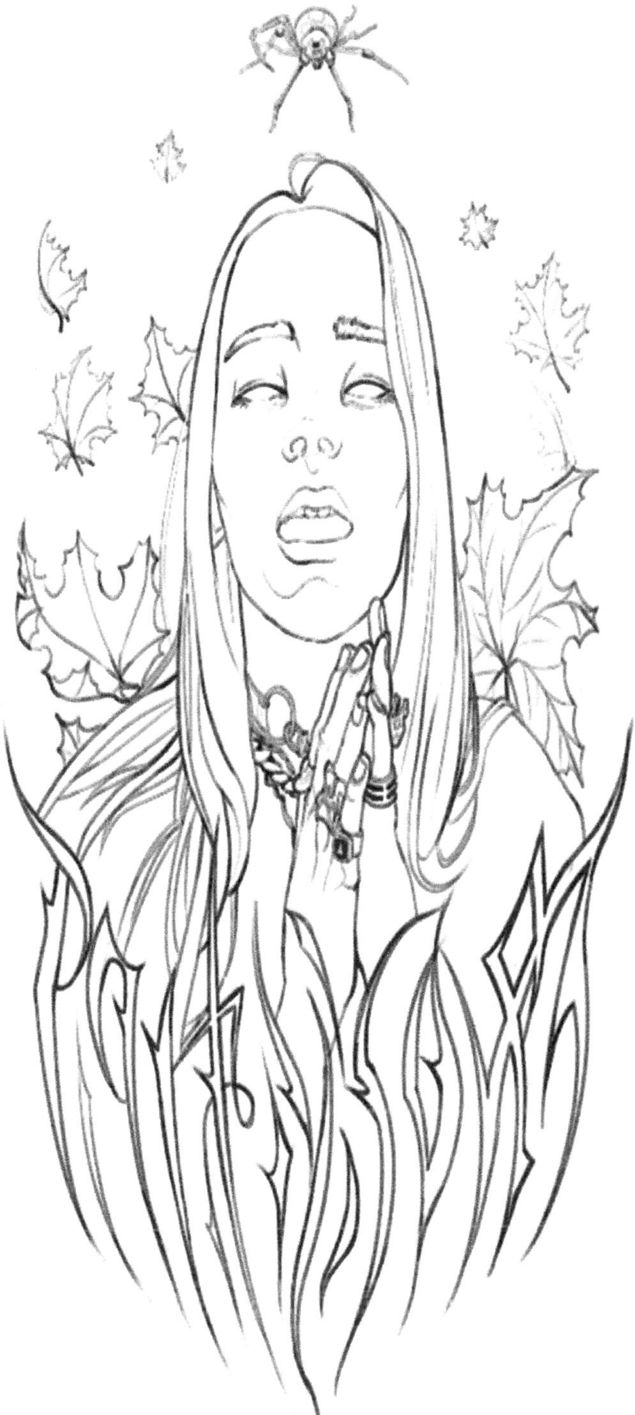

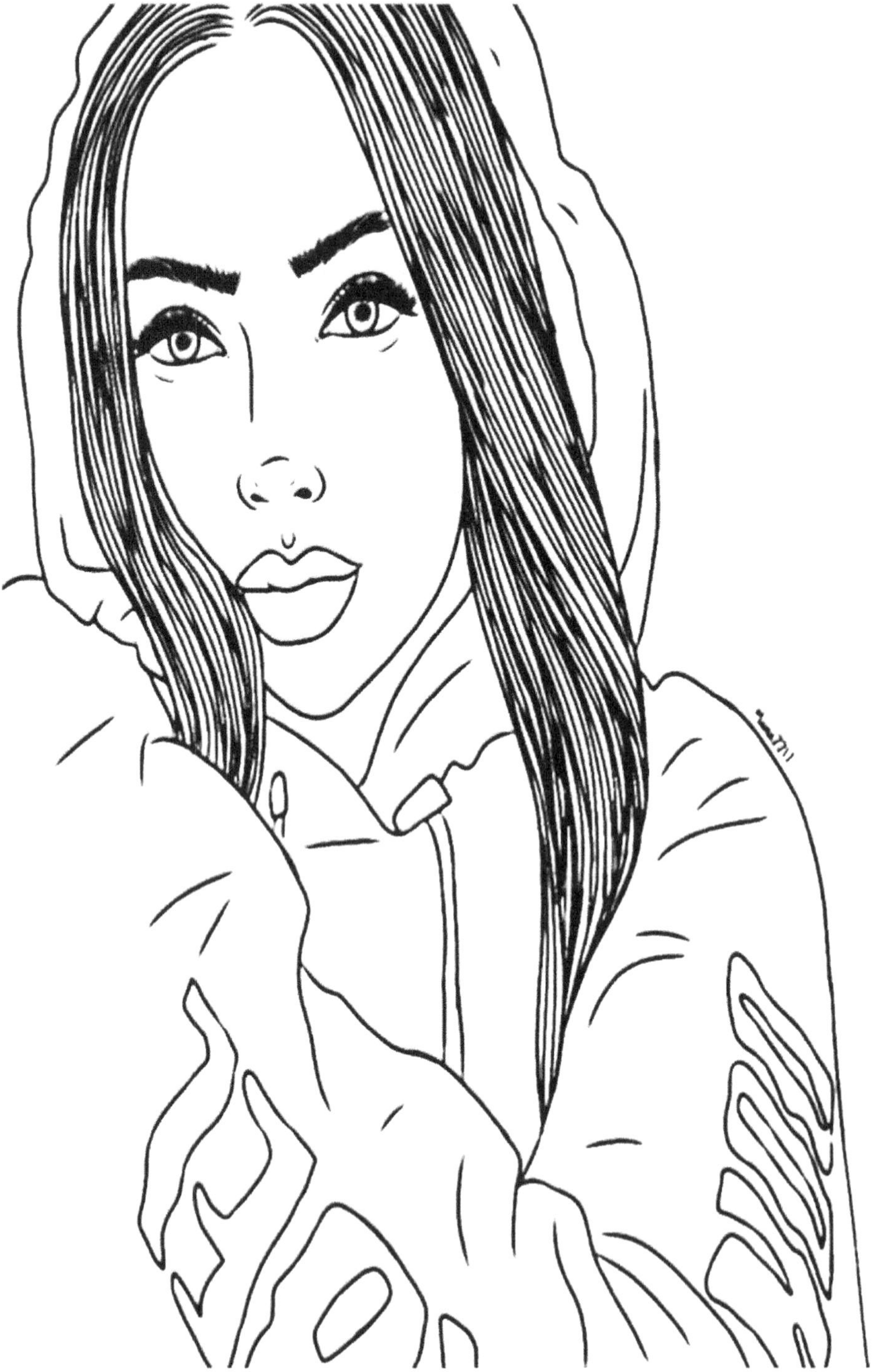

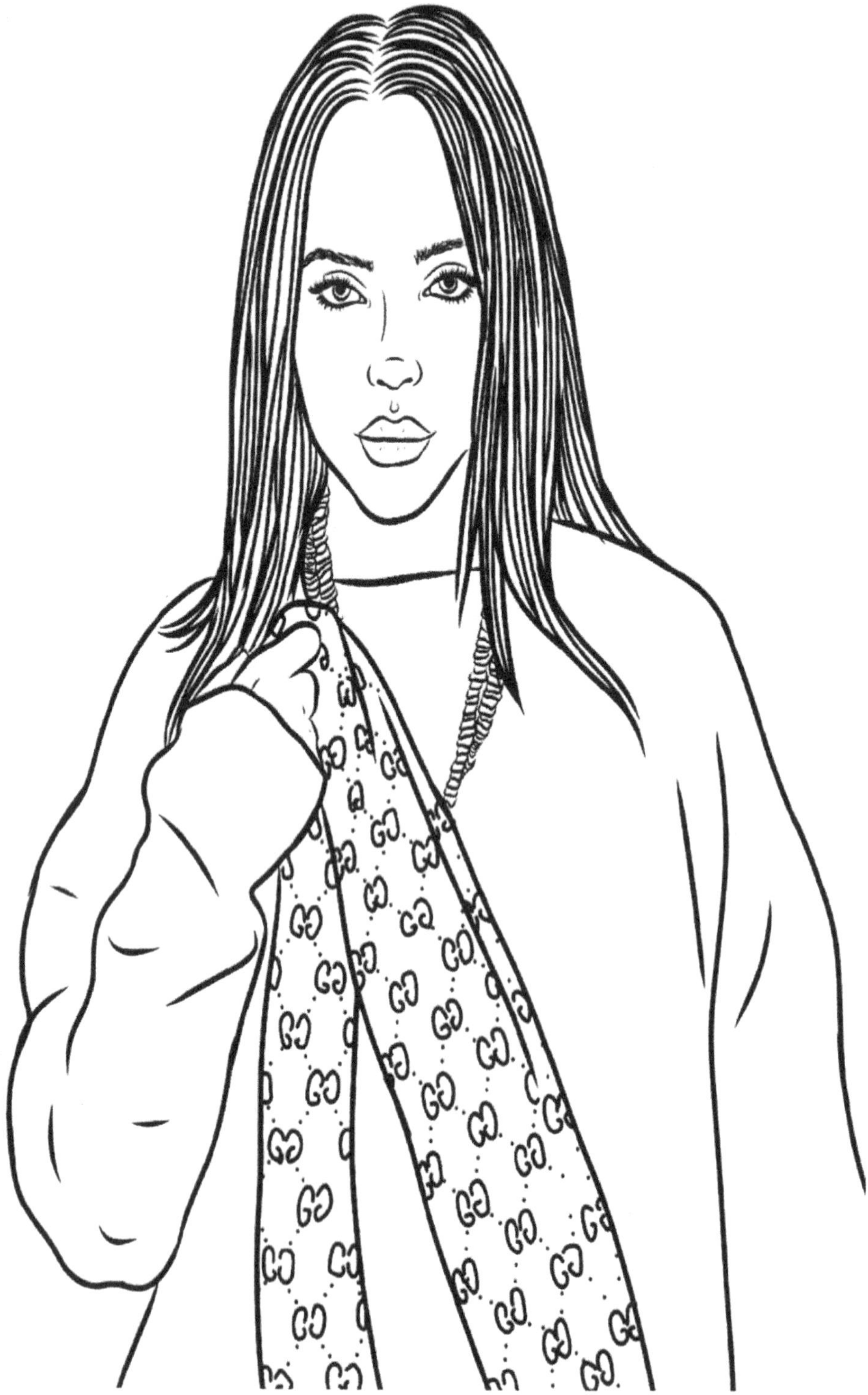

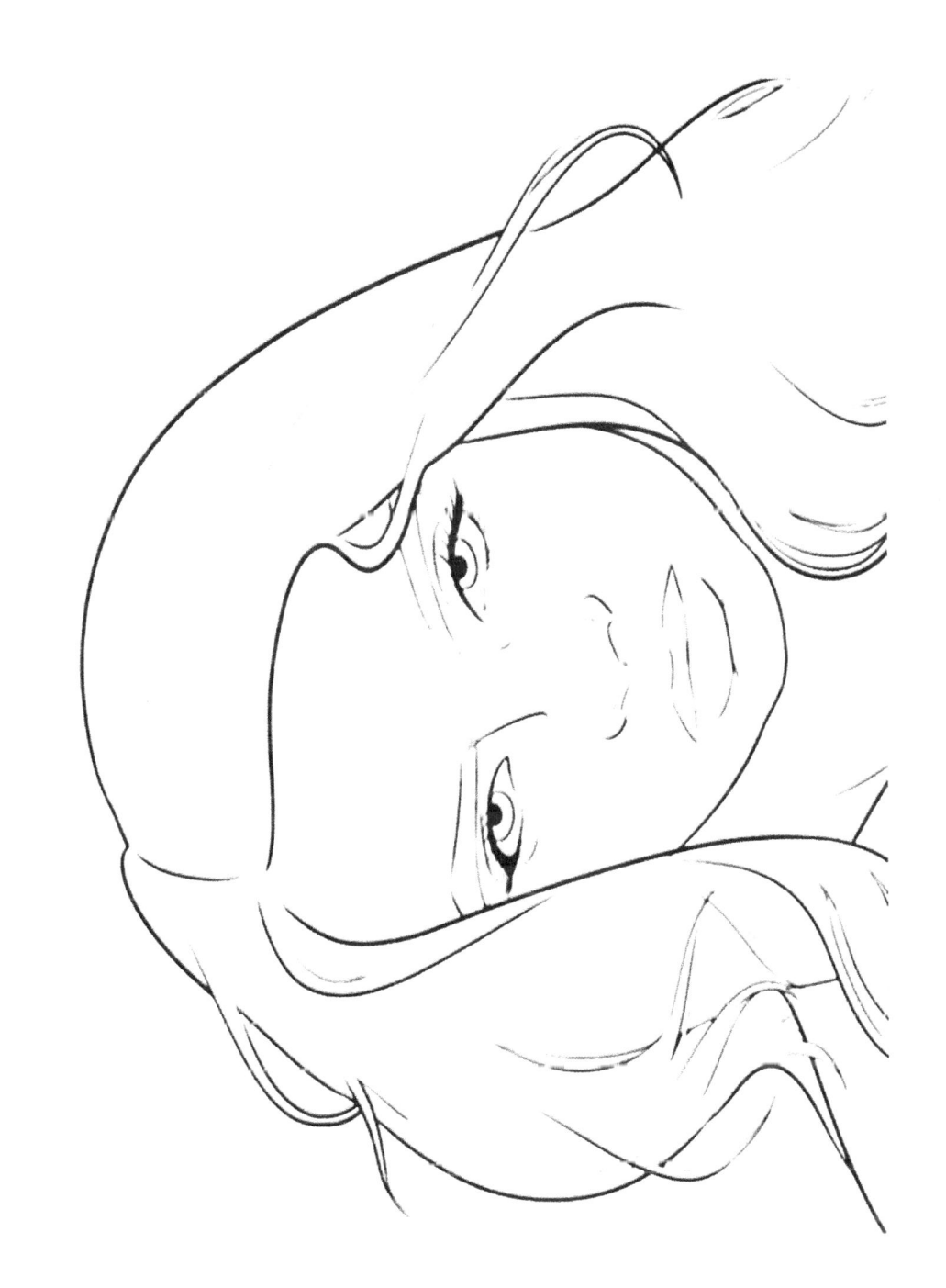

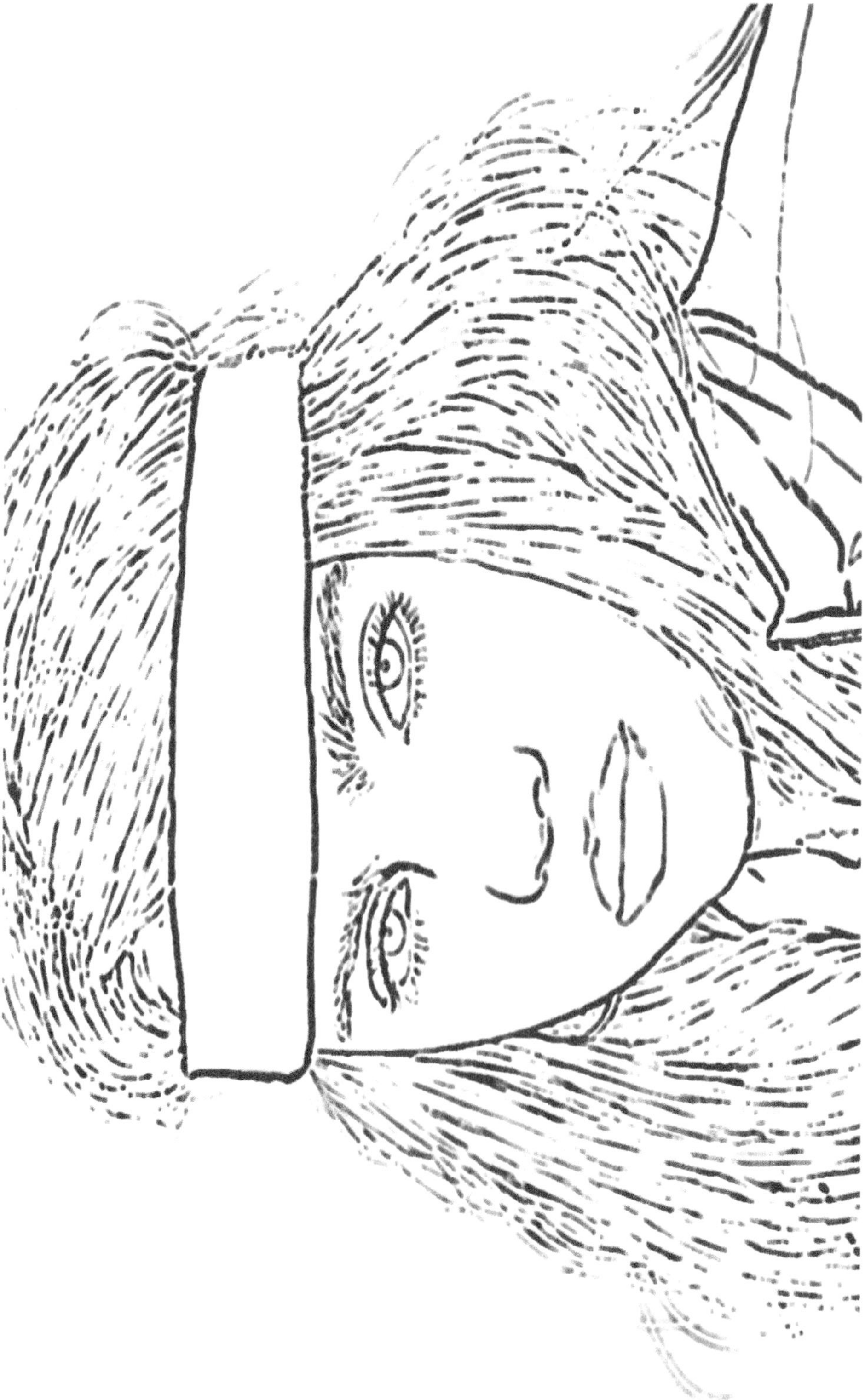

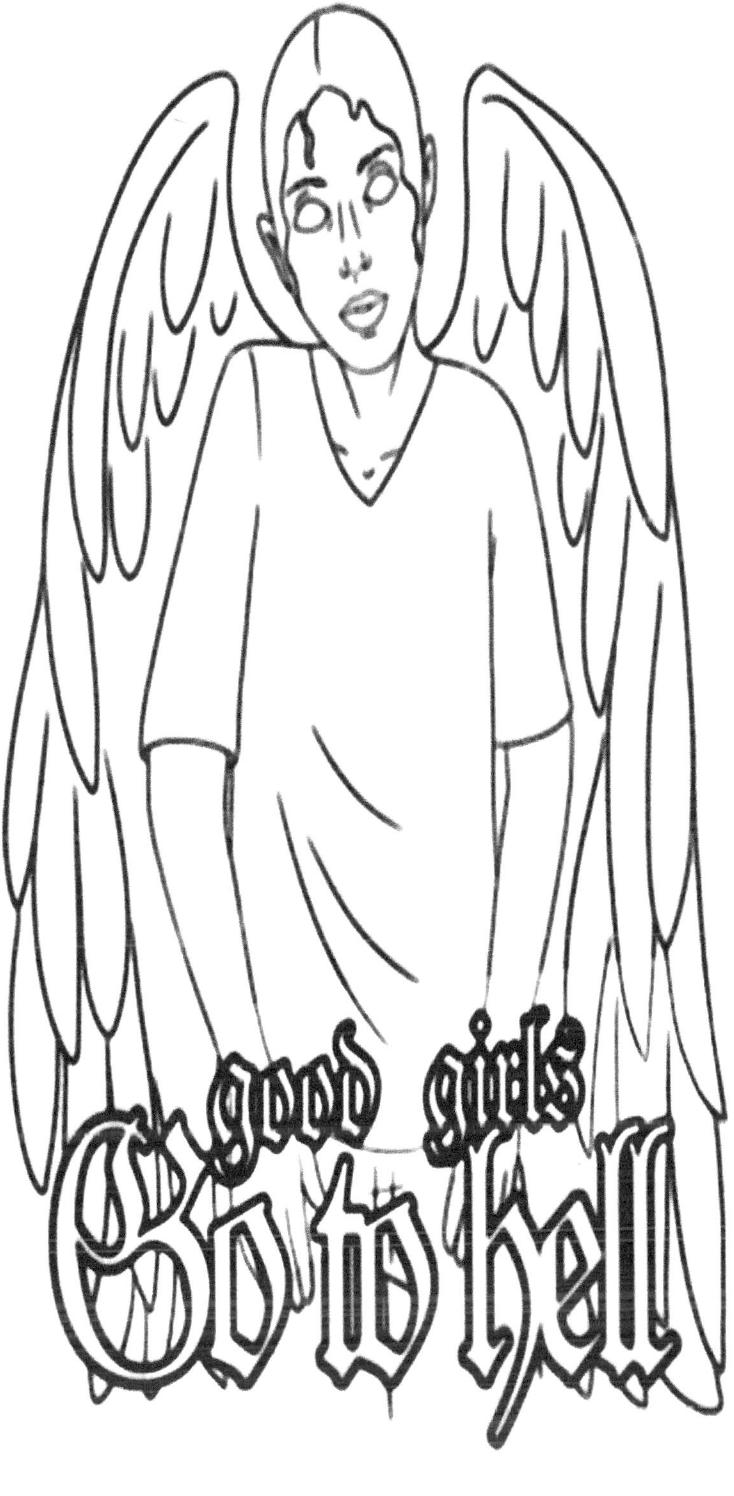
good girls
Go to hell

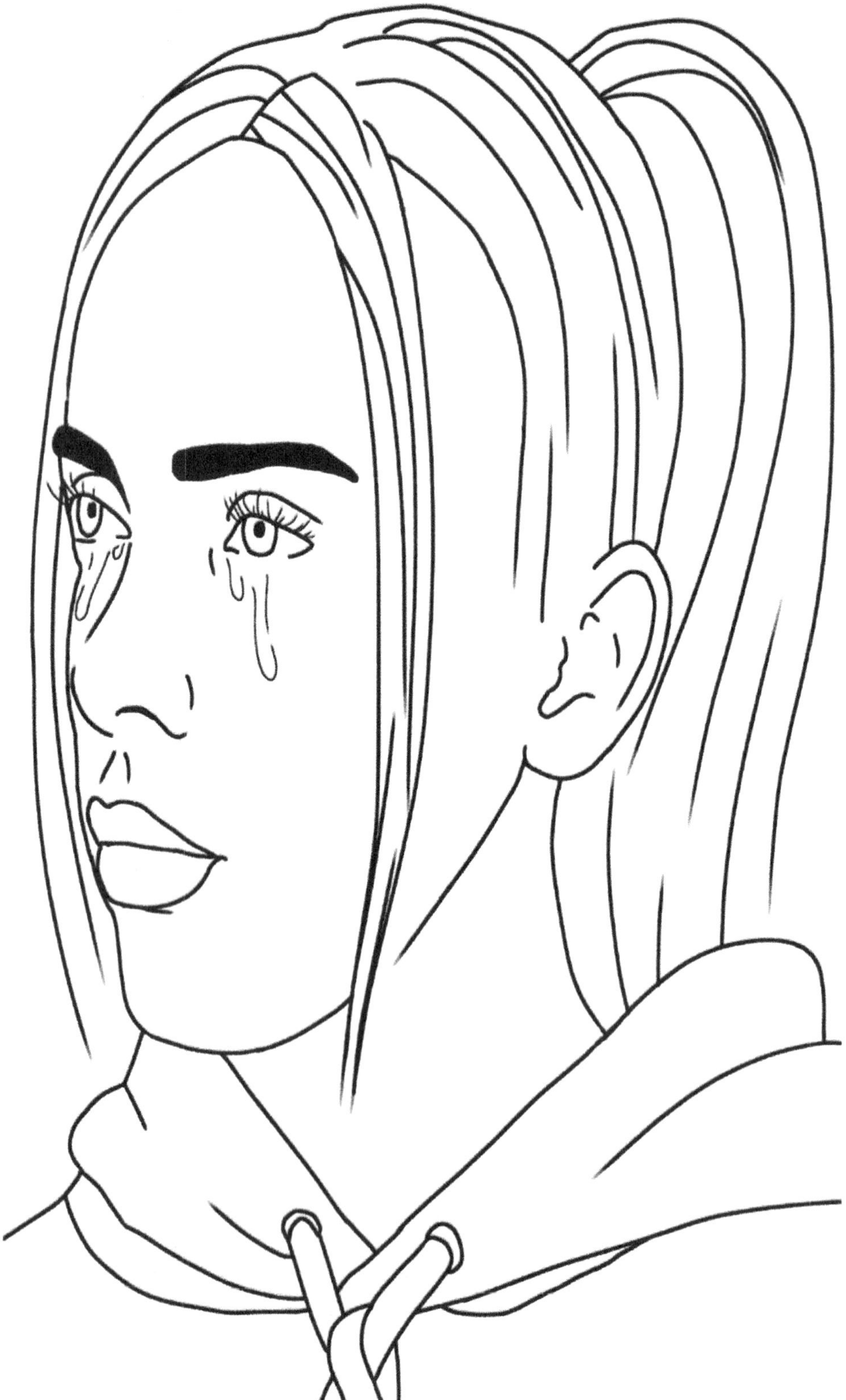

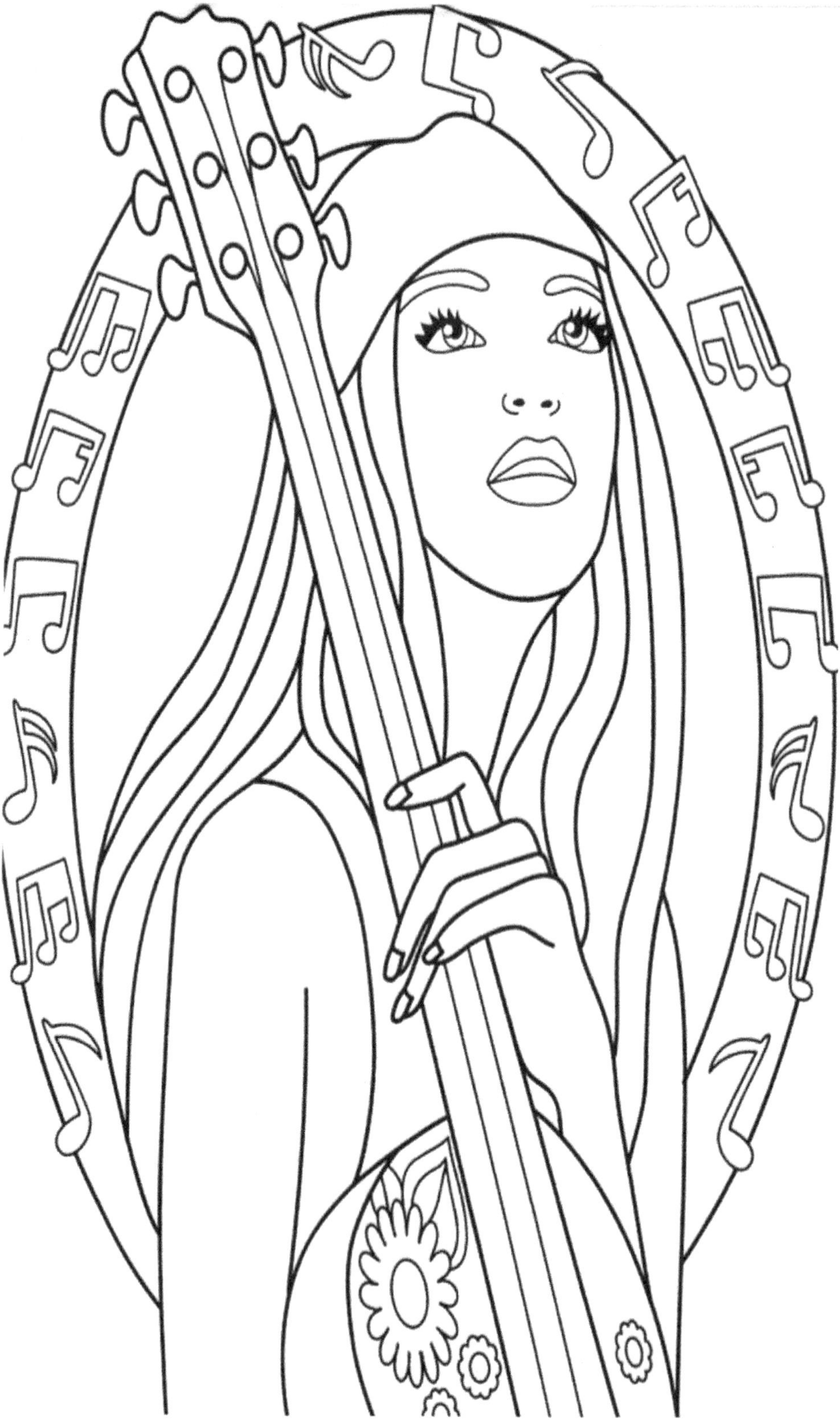

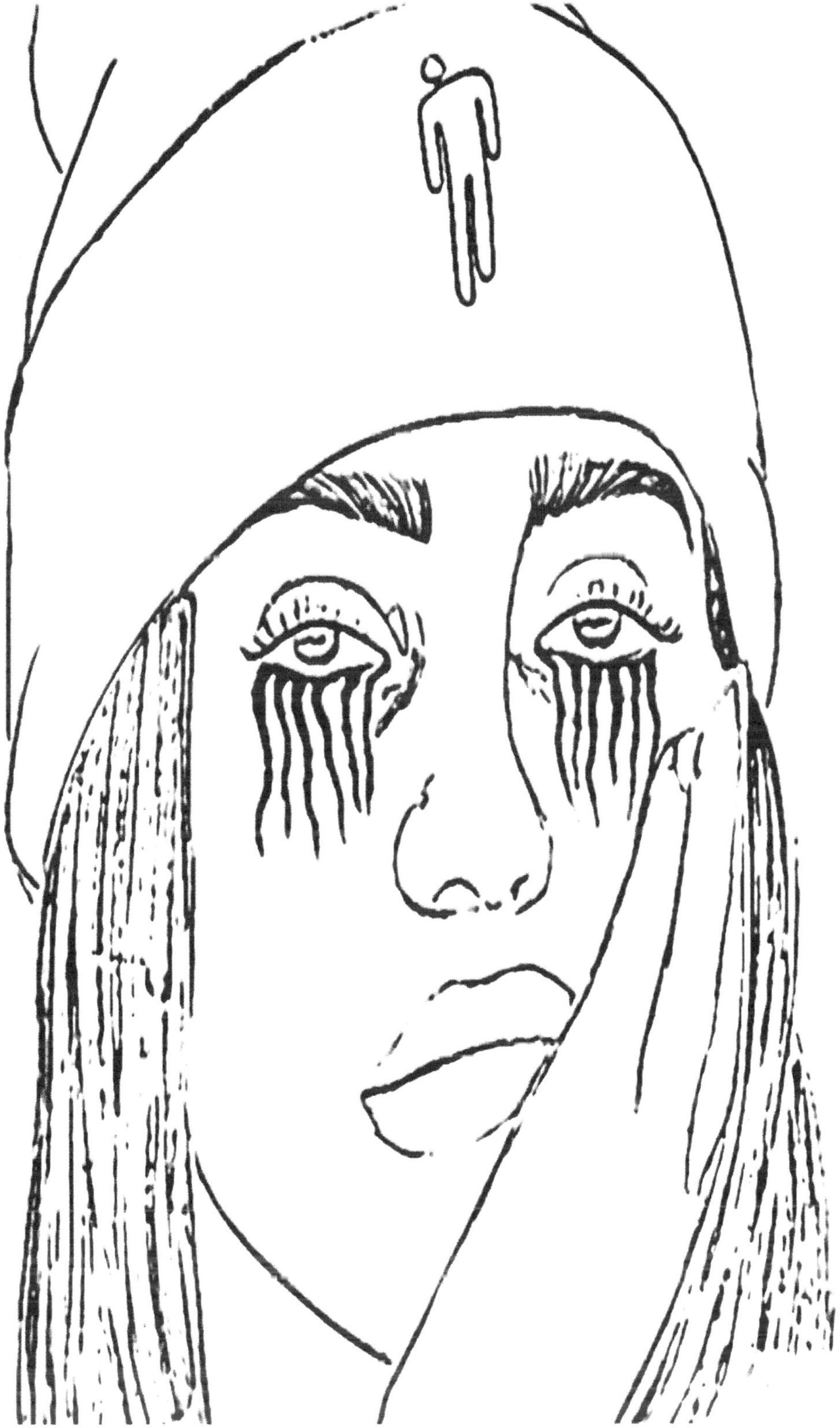

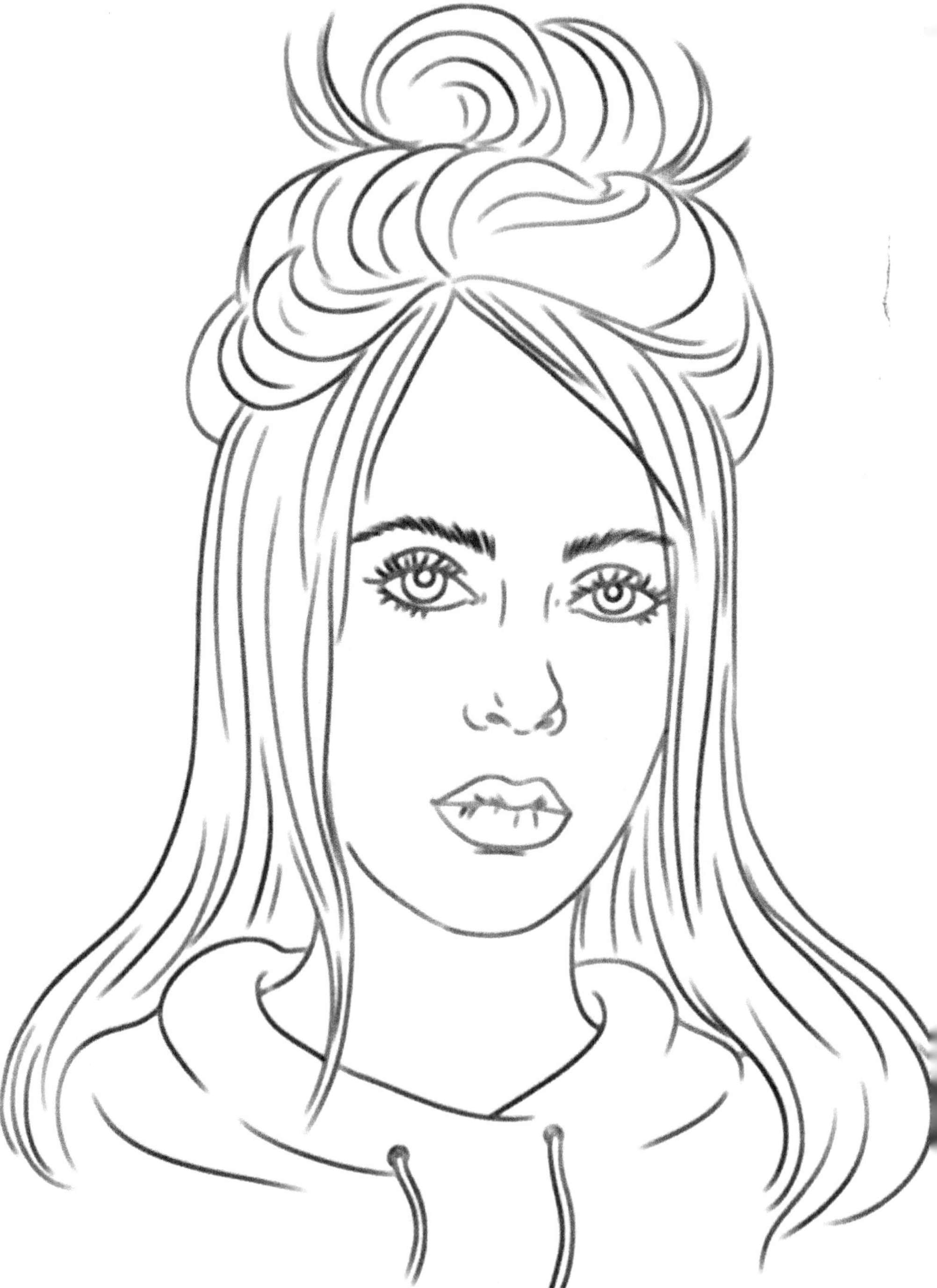

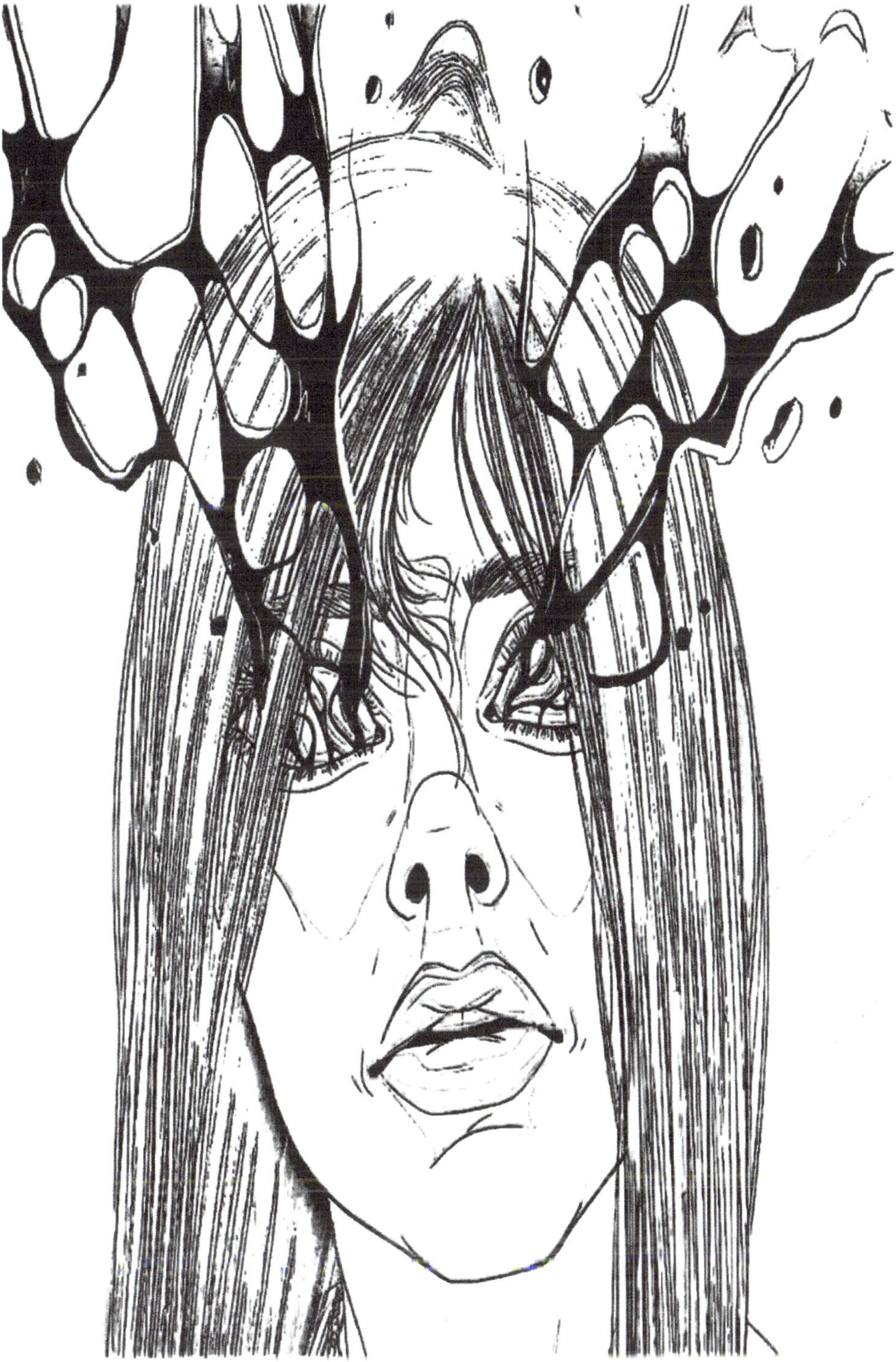

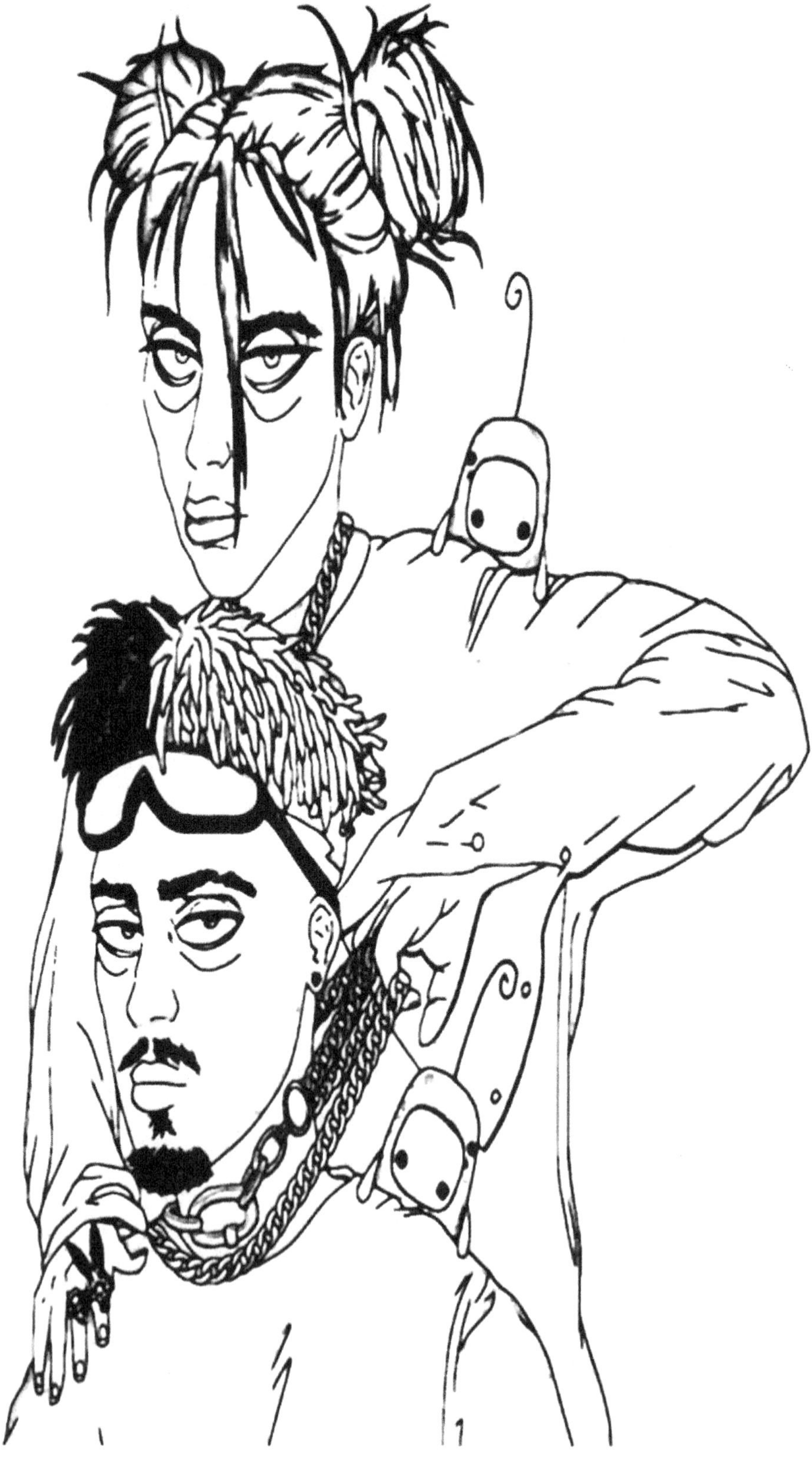

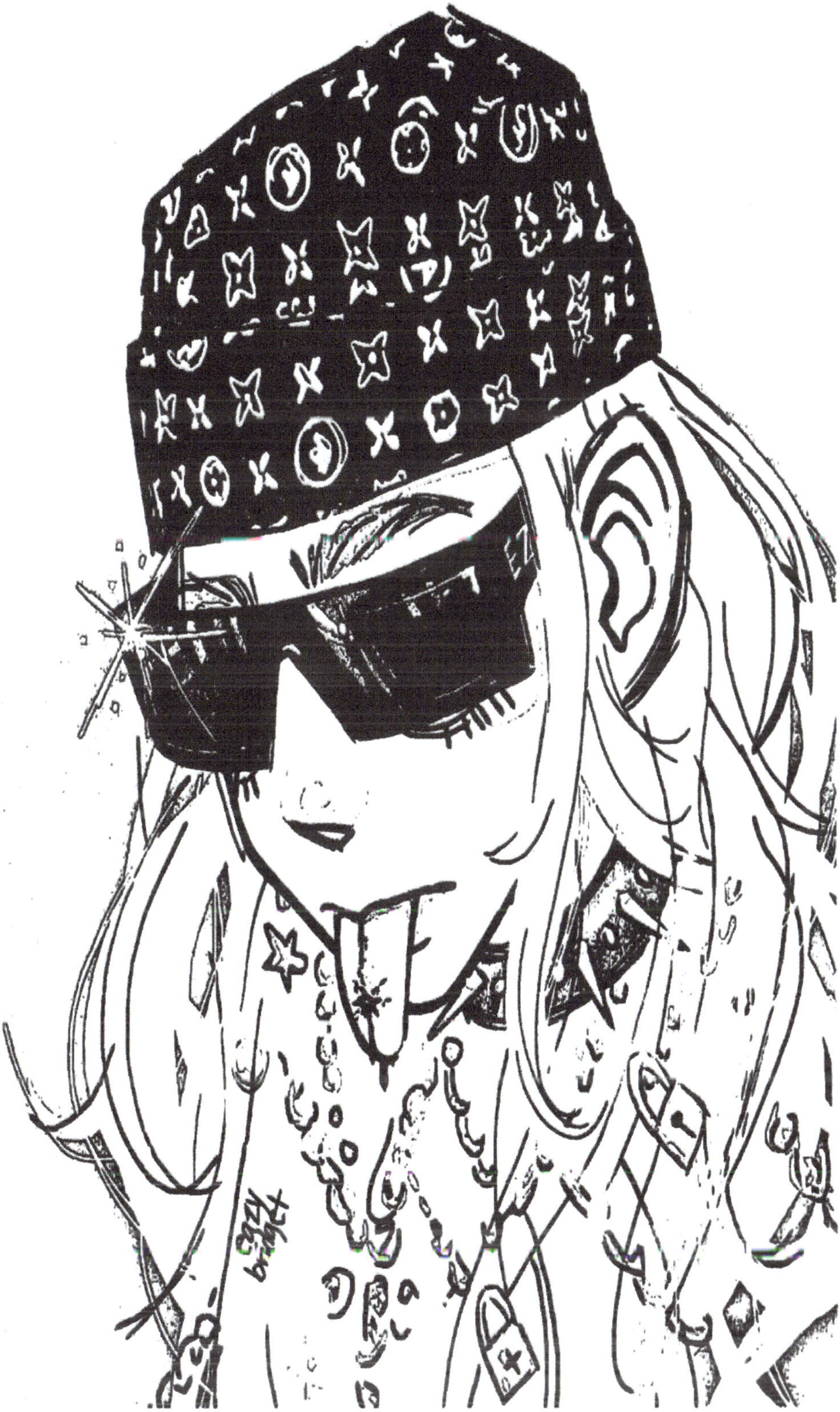

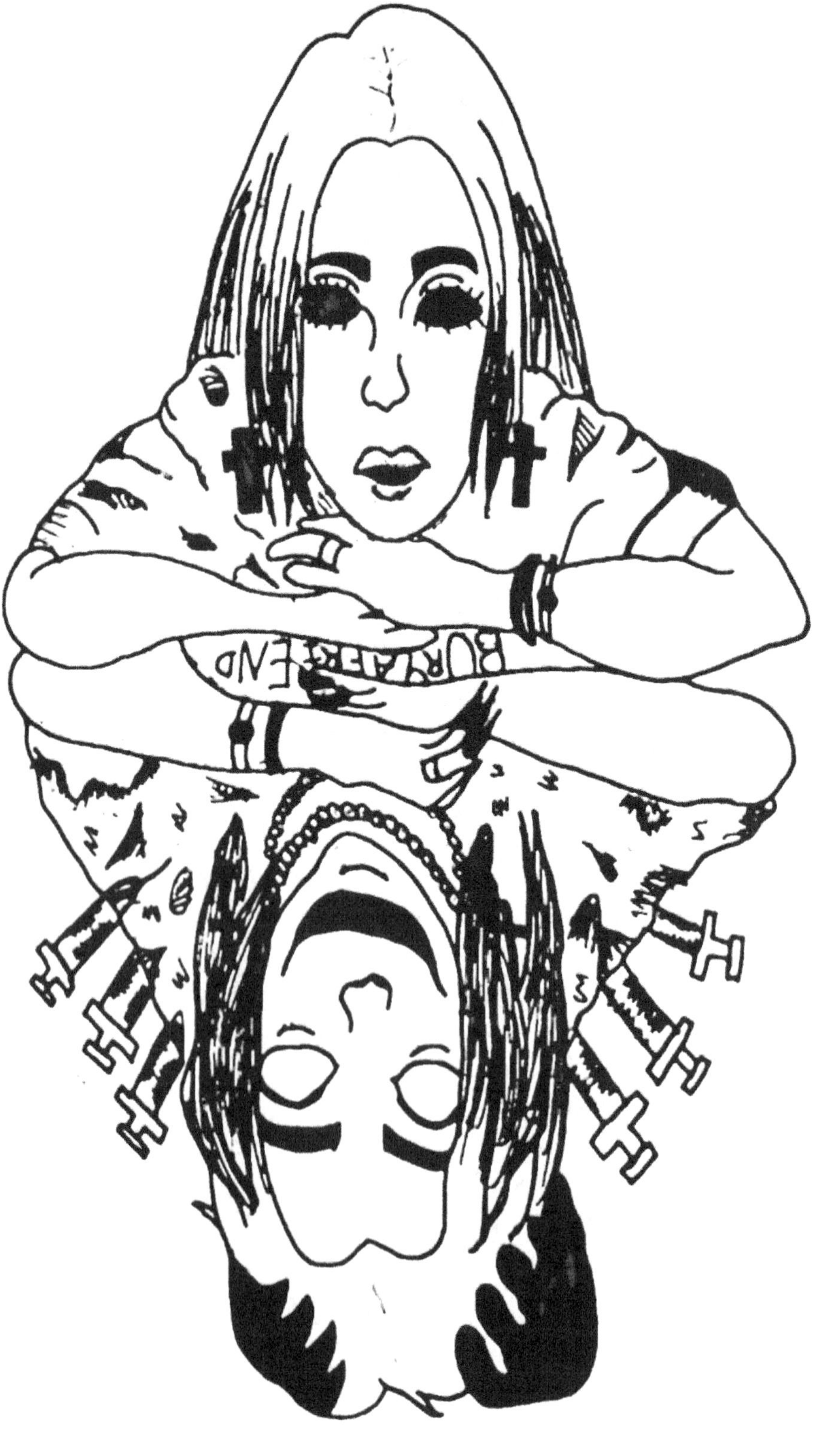

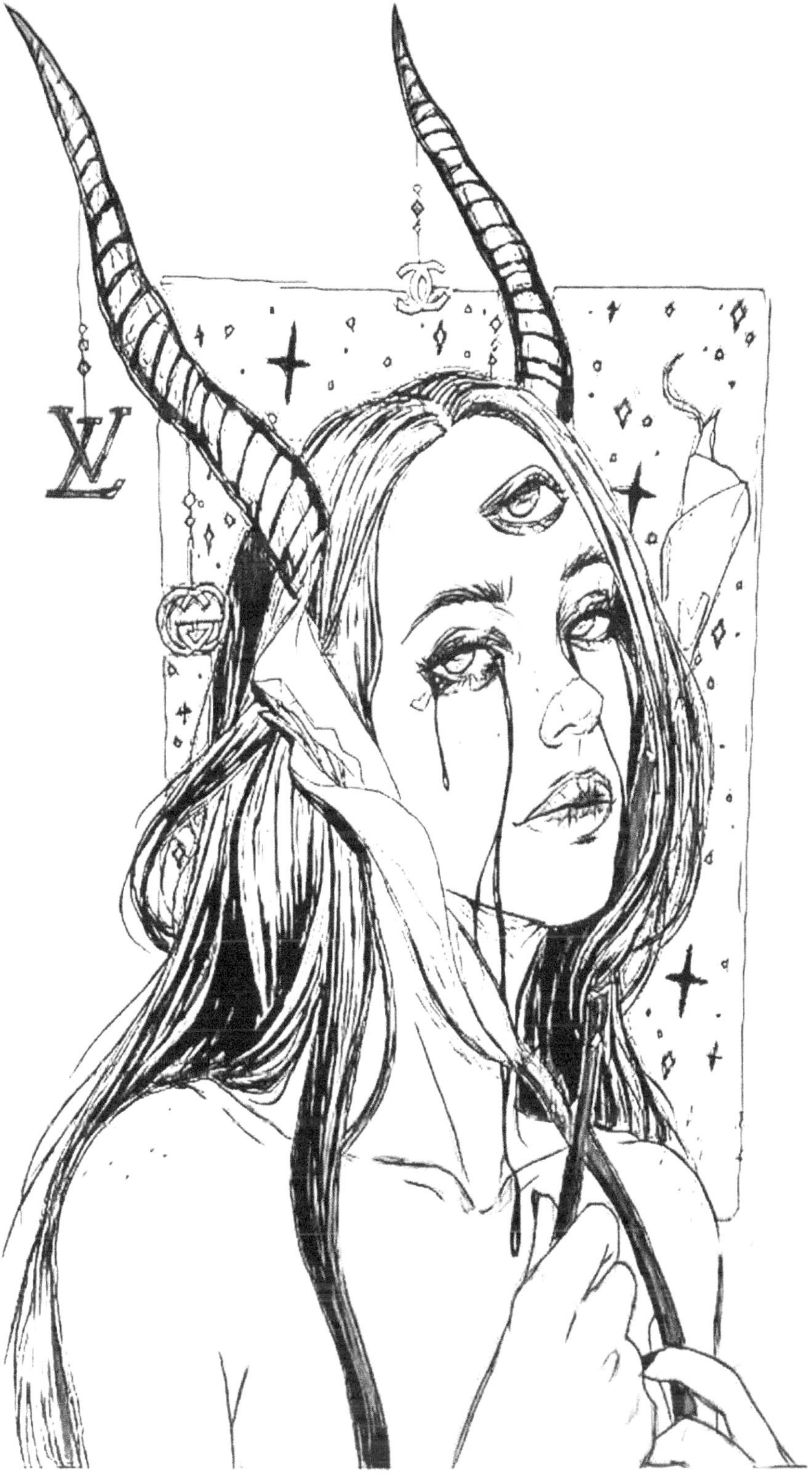

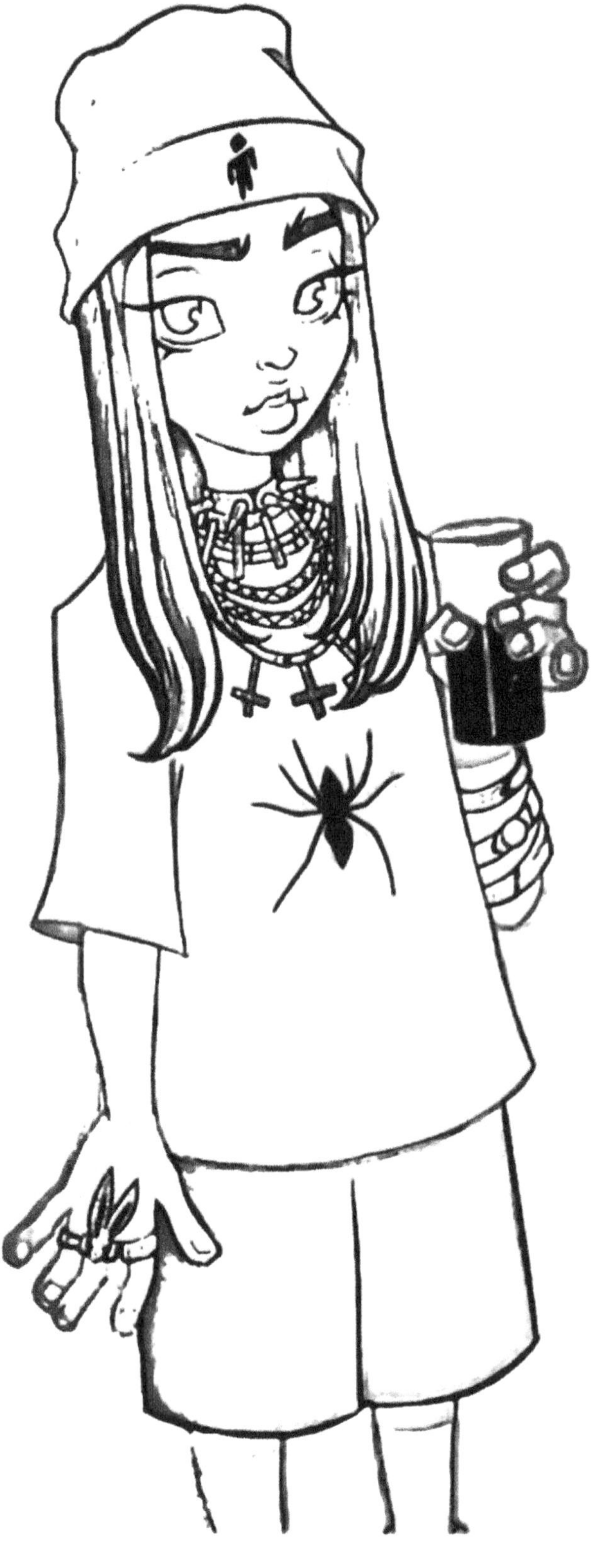

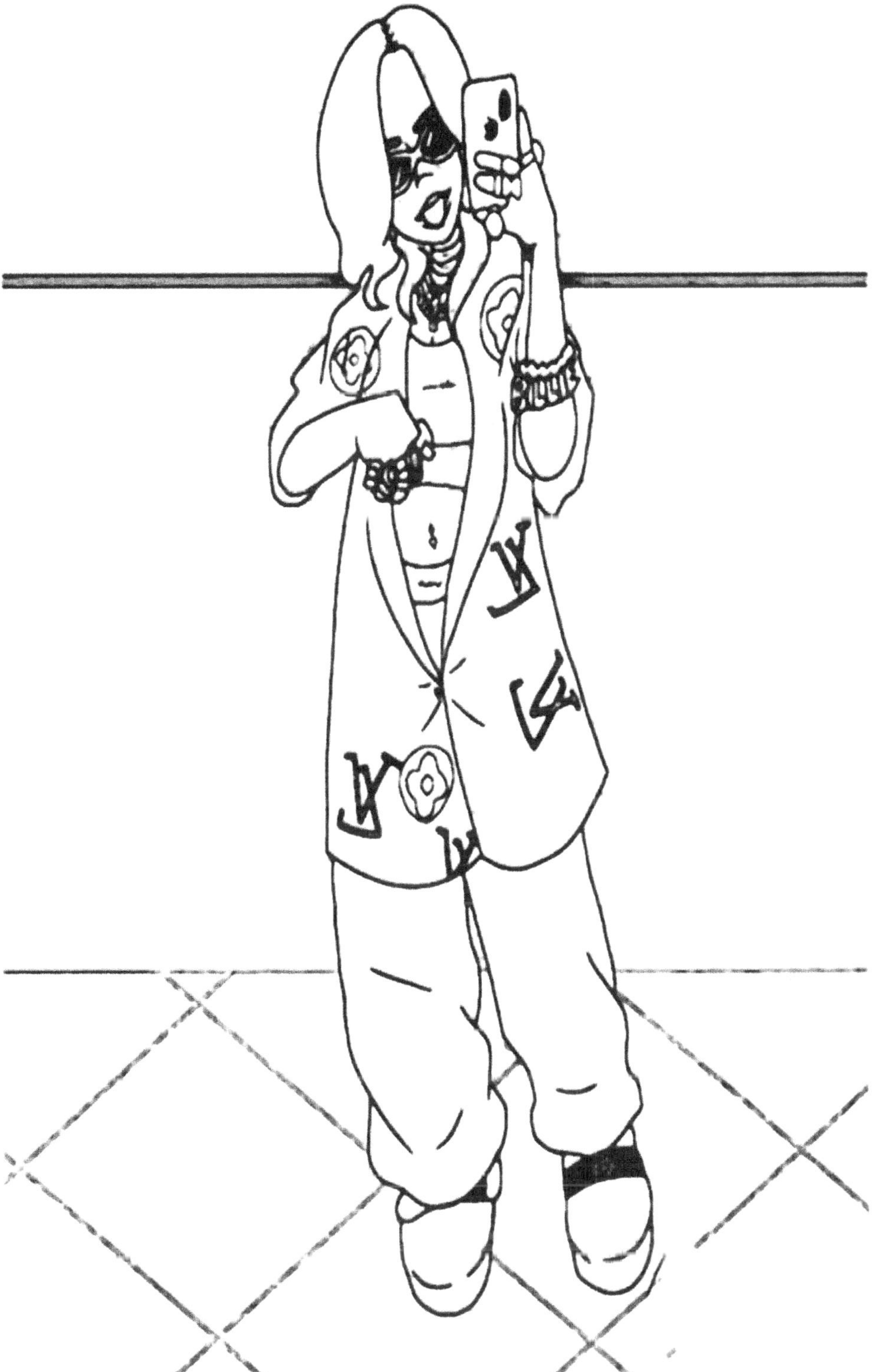

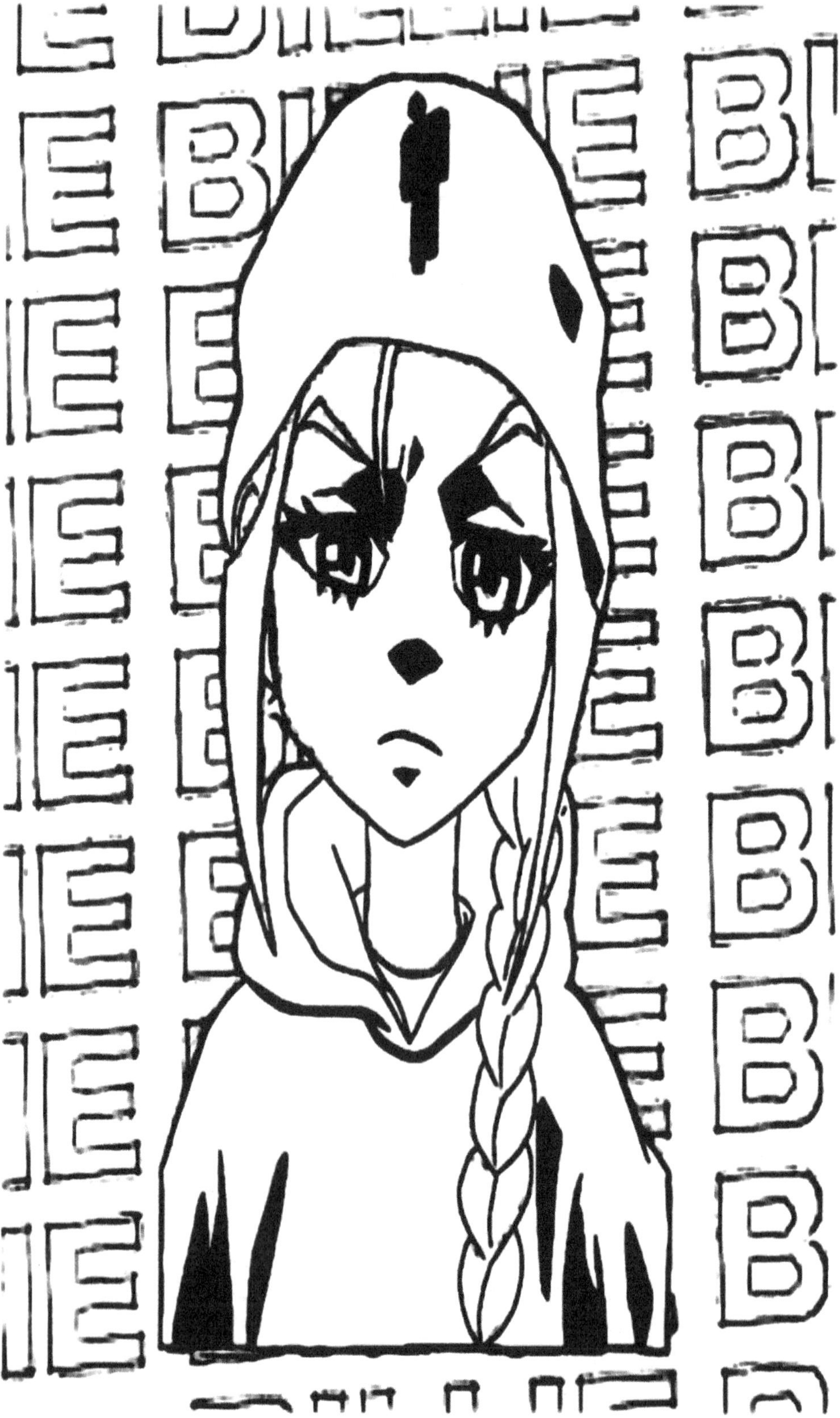

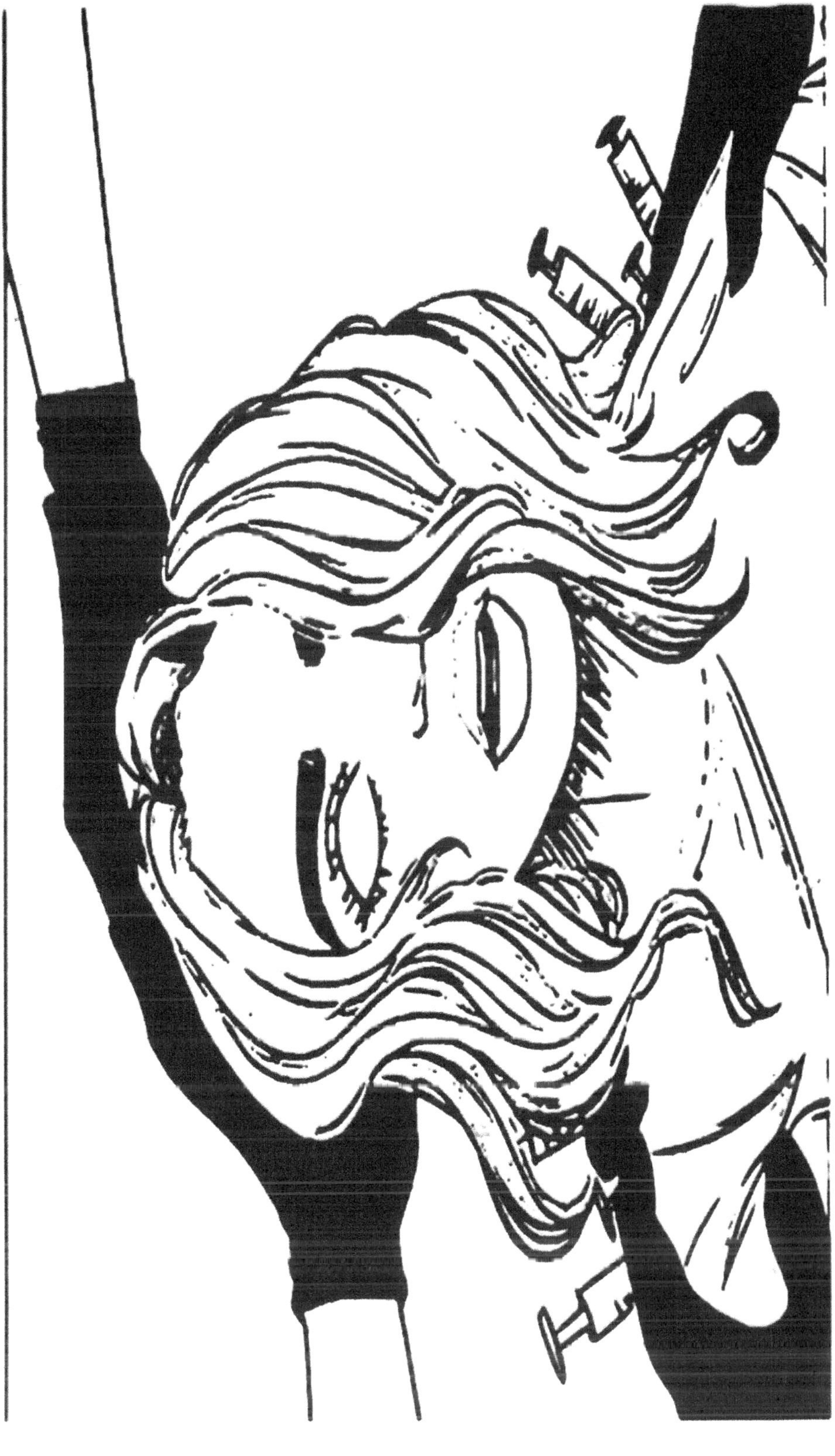

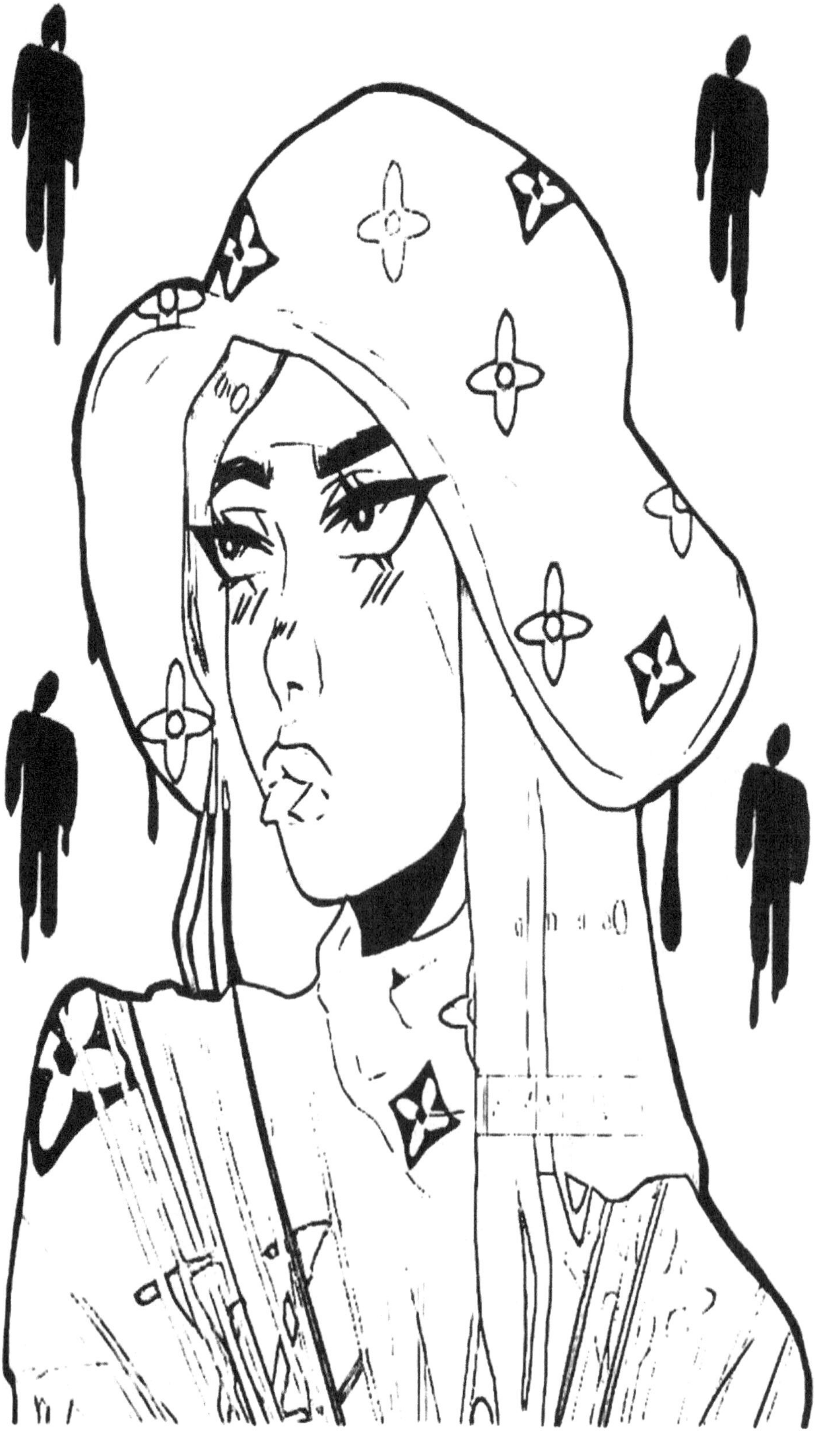

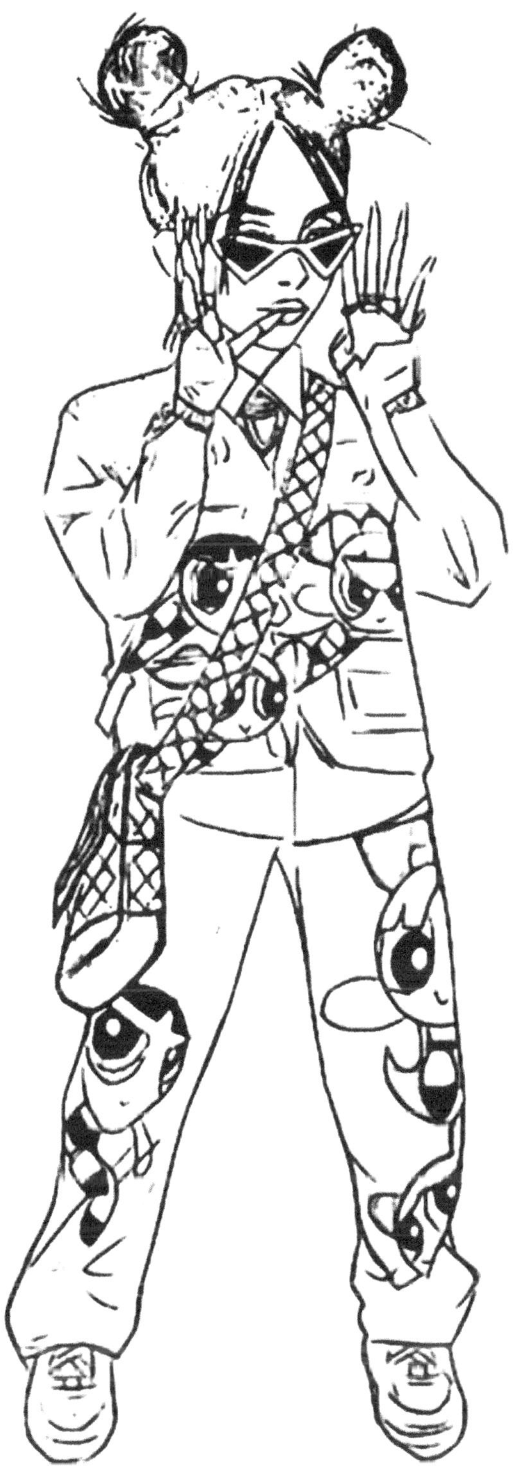

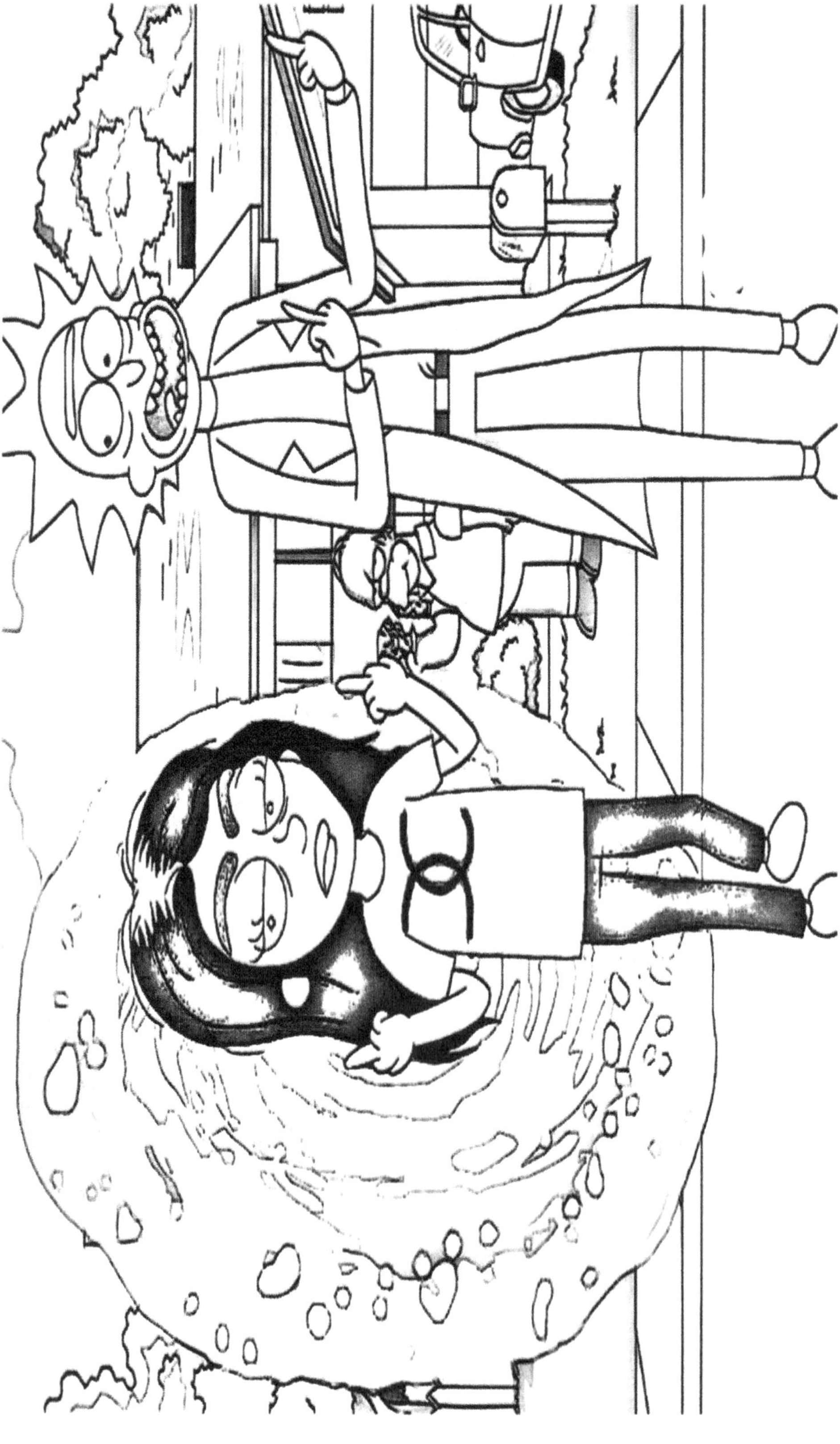

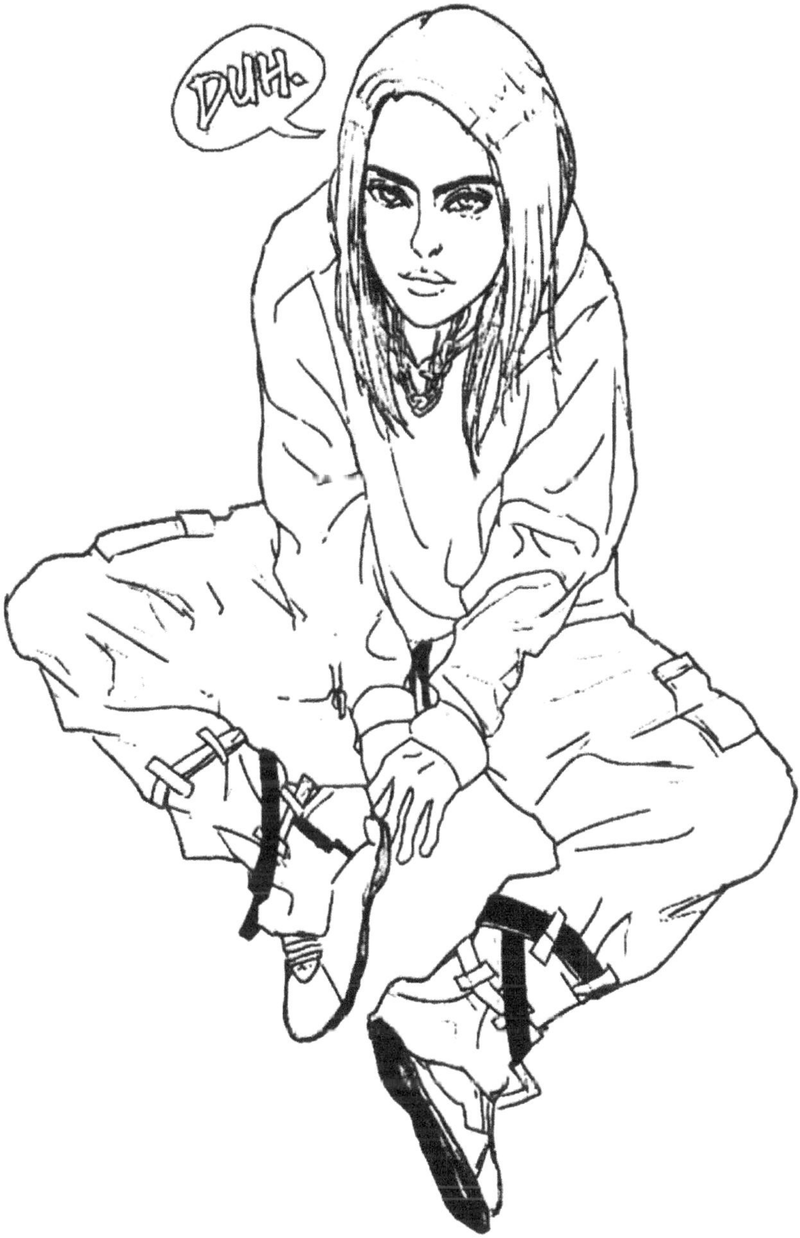
DUH.

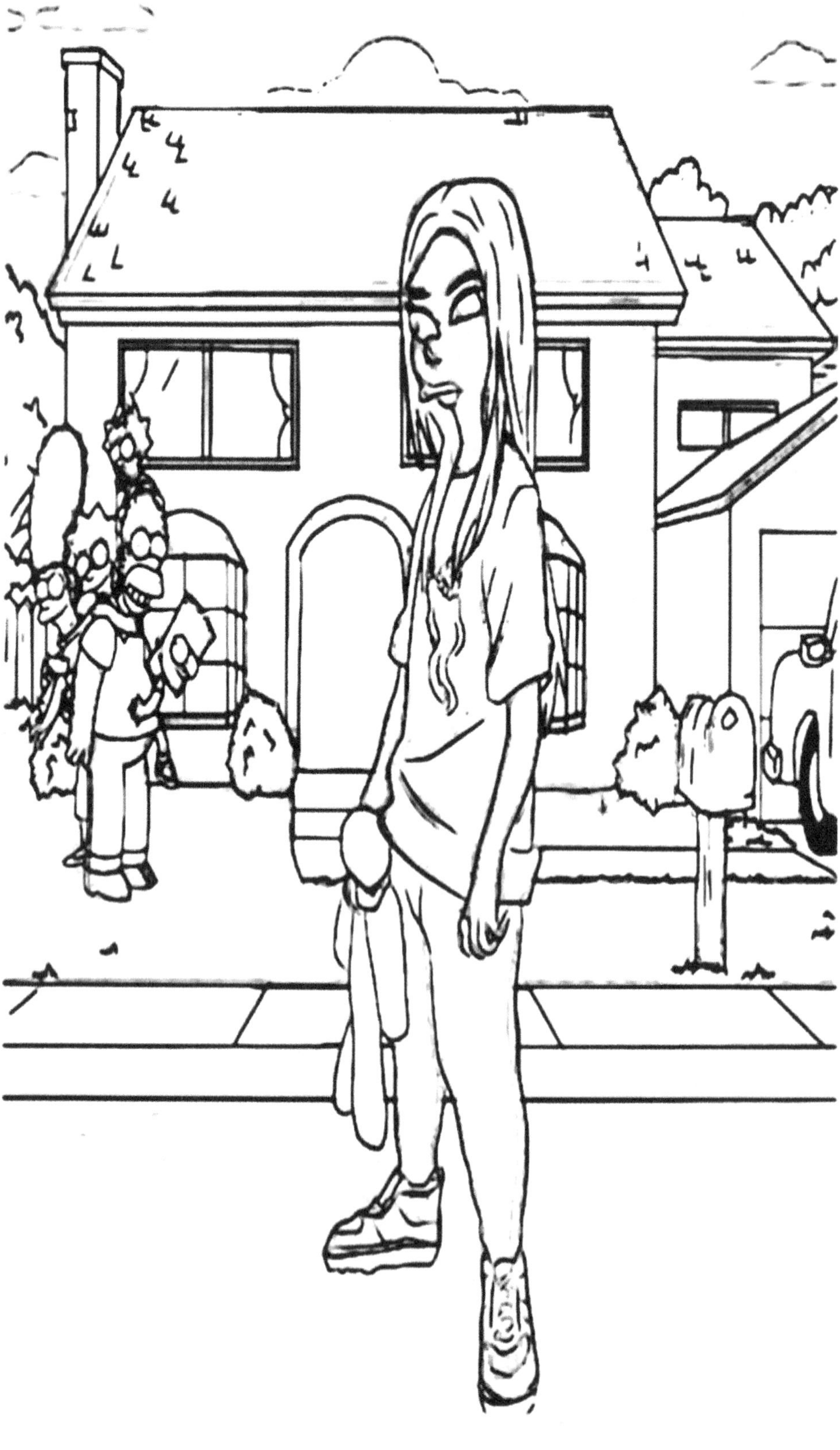

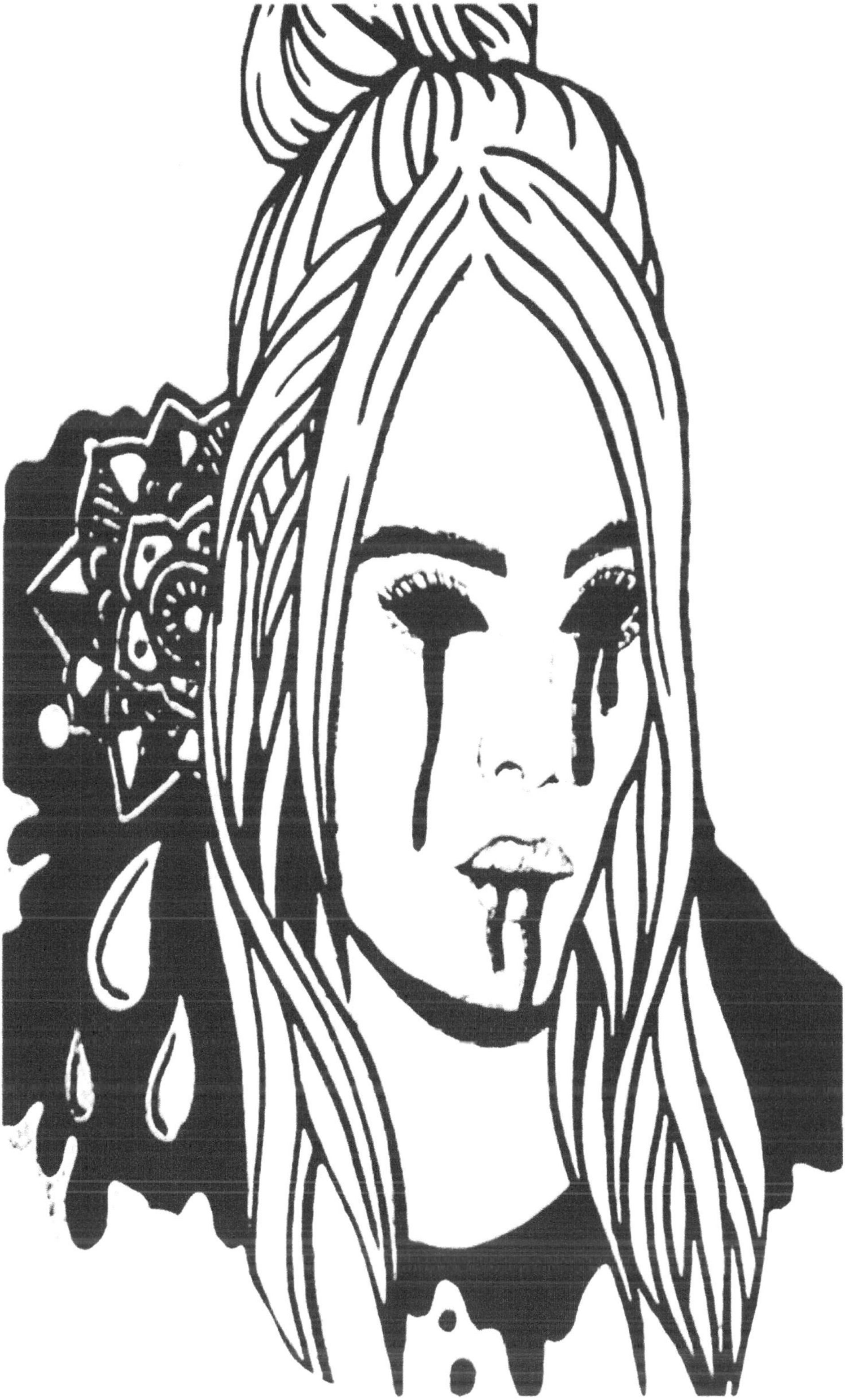

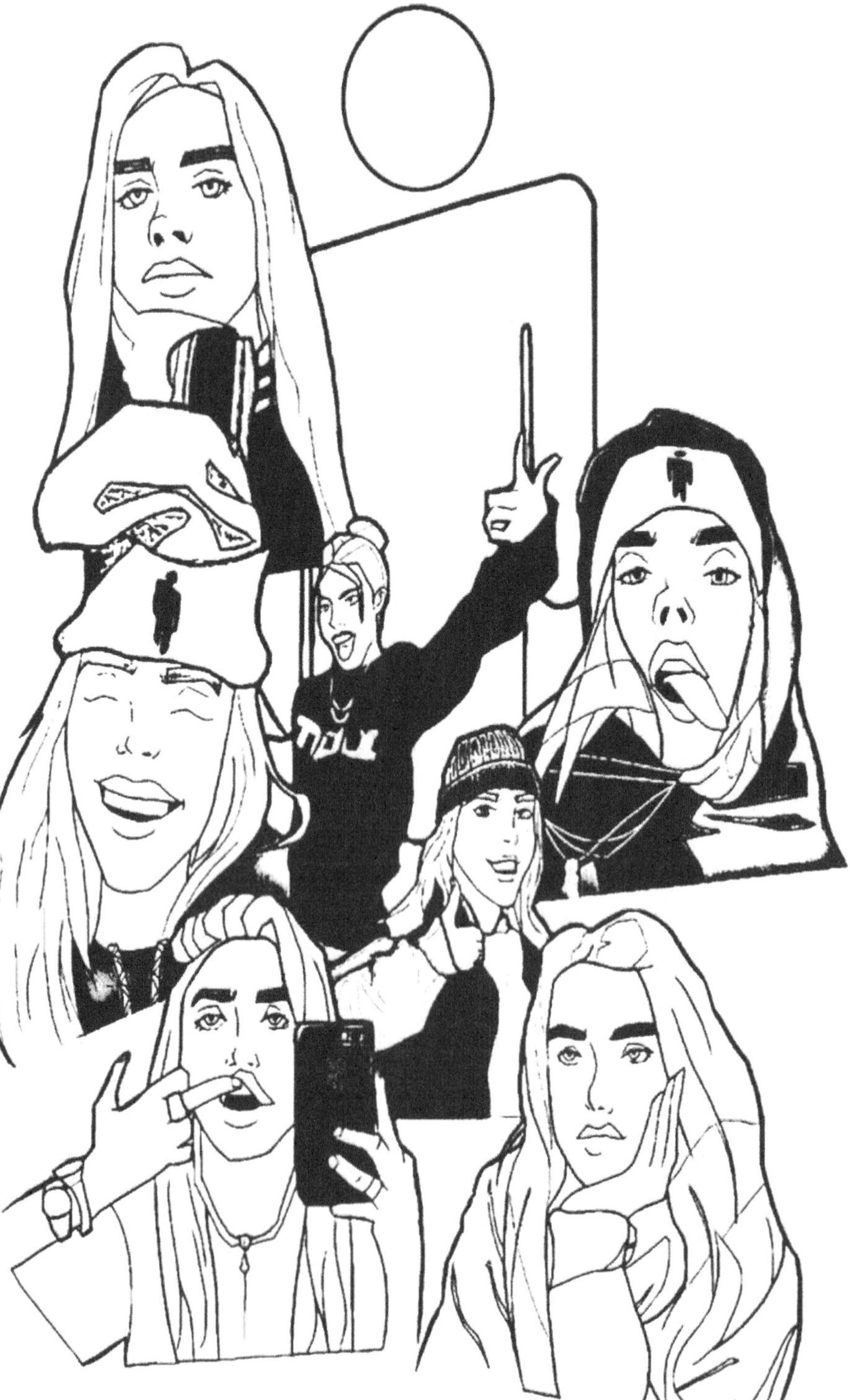

10% (ten percent) of our profits will be sent to a foundation that helps patients with cancer.

Please support us by only leaving 0 or 5 stars review rating on this book.

Thank you for buying this book, We hope you enjoyed coloring this book.

Made in the USA
Monee, IL
07 April 2020